and Pop Arranging

All

all

DARYL RUNSWICK

Dedicated to my father,
arranger extraordinary and my first teacher

I wish to thank James Wilson for his help in word-processing the manuscript of this book, and Wendy Thompson and Richard King, its editors.

© 1992 by Daryl Runswick
Daryl Runswick is hereby identified as author of this work in accordance with section 77 of the Copyright, Designs and Patents Act 1988

First published in 1992 by Faber Music Ltd
in association with Faber & Faber Ltd
3 Queen Square London WC1N 3AU
Design and typography by James Butler MCSD
Cover design by Shirley Tucker
Music and typesetting by Seton Music Graphics Ltd
Music examples hand-drawn by Paul Tyas
Printed in England by Caligraving Ltd
All rights reserved

ISBN 0-571-51108-2

To buy Faber Music publications or to find out about the full range of titles available please contact your local music retailer or Faber Music sales enquiries:

Faber Music Limited, Burnt Mill, Elizabeth Way, Harlow, CM20 2HX England
Tel: +44 (0)1279 82 89 82   Fax: +44 (0)1279 82 89 83
sales@fabermusic.com   www.fabermusic.com

Contents

Introduction

When you buy a new cassette-player, synth or fx (effects) box, it comes with a manual. How many times have you groaned at the words 'It is important to read all the instructions before operating the equipment'? Well, this manual is different.

You are hereby *forbidden* to waste your time trying to get this whole book into your head before you start the real job of putting musical ideas into action. There's no need: you can operate this equipment now. YOU KNOW ENOUGH ALREADY to do good arrangements.

And on the other hand, naturally, there are things – techniques, methods, info – that you may need to access as you become an experienced arranger. That's what this book is for.

It is laid out so that you can get to single bits of information quickly, without having to wade through oceans of text. It will tell you how to write out a drum part or a chord sheet, what notes you can and cannot write for a sax or a violin, how to use the various sounds on a synth, how to do a 'routine' for a song or number, and much more.

It's a mixture of solid facts and recommendations based on experience. The facts you should obey; the recommendations you can take or leave. They work, as it happens. But you may have better ideas than me. Times change, and so do fashions. Madonna didn't get where she did by following the recommendations of Diana Ross.

How to use this book

1 **To get a fact** (e.g., how do I write a trumpet part?)
Flip through the book until you find the chapter you need (e.g. Brass and Reeds, Chapter 10).

Go through the section headings until you find the right topic (e.g. 'Trumpet').

Run your finger down the subheadings until you come to the precise info.

The info is given twice within each numbered paragraph: once in brief, so that the next time the problem comes up you can quickly remind yourself; and a second time more fully, to give you all the detail you need.

OR there's an index at the back of the book.

2 **To learn a technique** (e.g., how do I use ℀ to save myself paper and effort?)
This requires a greater amount of reading through sections, but even here the layout helps.

Find the subject you want by using the index or by flipping through the book.

The brief info at the start of each paragraph will tell you whether you need to read the detail or can skip on.

Later, when you're re-reading to remind yourself, the brief info will often be all you'll need.

3 **To lay out a page of music**
There's a sample page of music near the beginning of most of the chapters. (Chapter 1's is a little way in.)

So, you can check what a lead sheet looks like by turning to Chapter 1.

You can check out a trumpet part by looking at Chapter 10.

You can look at a complete score in Chapter 15.

And so on.

Often a glance at one of these pages will remind you of a fact or technique you've half-forgotten, and save you the bother of looking it up.

4 **Cross-referencing**
If a word has (*) after it, there's a section on it somewhere in the book. Look in the index.

5 **Glossary**
If you don't understand a word, look it up in the Glossary. Most things are explained there – BUT I do assume you can read music. I don't explain crotchets and bass clefs.
 More difficult musical terms *are* explained.

Incidentals

1 **Program/programme.** In computer language (and therefore the language of synths) the spelling is program. If you go to a concert in Great Britain, however, you read the programme. I have observed this difference in the book.

2 **Gender.** The book is intended to be gender-neutral. Sentences like 'Every player has his own style' don't exist here. At the very beginning I set my word processor to print 'her or his' every time a case like that came up.

A note to the professional

In the past the method adopted in many arranging and orchestration textbooks has been to work up from an exhaustive treatment of details (instrument ranges, transpositions, etc.) through examples and discussions of techniques for combining small groups of instruments, to a final section demonstrating various types of full score. This, which we might call the theoretical method, has disadvantages for the book's users, involving as it too often does long swathes of text in which the need for information-retrieval is subordinated to the flow of the author's argument.

I have tried to write a different kind of book. Nine times out of ten my users will have a group or band they want to write for, and a song or tune they want to arrange. They will also, *always,* have some existing expertise, if only in the form of tastes and intentions. (These intentions, incidentally, cannot be known by me; and the older the book becomes, the less relevant any stylistic exhortations will be.)

The users of the book I have envisaged will use it to supplement their embryonic expertise: they will want specific bits of information in a quickly retrievable form, separable from other, unwanted information. If, in addition, they can be given a context and layout in which useful facts catch their eye as they search, so much the better.

Ideally the index of such a book would show one page reference only for each subject! I have of course failed in that aim.

The Routine :
The Lead Sheet

OK – straight in at the deep end. You have a tune or a song; perhaps you wrote it yourself, perhaps you didn't.

You'll need an overall shape for your arrangement. This is called a **routine**.

Then you'll need to write out the arrangement in the shortest way that will give people all the basic info about it. This is called a **lead sheet**.

This chapter is in the form of a tutorial to teach you these techniques step by step.

At the end of the chapter there's a section called 'Overview' which is all you'll need to glance at after you've done one or two arrangements.

Tutorial 1: Routining a cover version

1 **The first arrangement you ever tried to do was probably a straight copy of a favourite record.**
Professionals call a straight copy a cover version. You didn't need to *make* a routine – you already had one, the record itself. Now, you may have thought of it as simply a great record. Something whole and complete. But . . .

2 **When that tune was being recorded,** *someone routined it!*
They decided whether there was to be an intro; which verses would get repeated; where any instrumental breaks would go; whether there would be backing vocals (*) (bvox); what synths or guitars would play; etc., etc.

3 **It's good exercise (and fun) to take a record and strip the routine down to its bare essentials.**
What song does nearly everybody know? 'Memory' from *Cats*. OK, it's old hat, but like it or loathe it, you probably know it, so I can use it as an example. (I also have permission from the publisher to use it.) I'm talking below about Elaine Paige's record of the song.

4 See if it's possible to divide up the song into sections which you can label 'a', 'b', 'c', etc., plus introduction, any instrumental breaks, and ending.

5 Midnight, not a sound from the pavement
Has the moon lost her memory
In the lamp-light the withered leaves collect at my feet
And the wind begins to moan.

On the record there's a four-bar orchestral **introduction** and then the verse. So start a table.

	Intro	four bars B♭ major, $\frac{12}{8}$ time
a	Verse 1	eight bars (of curious lengths! see **24** below)

6 Memory, all alone in the moonlight
I can smile at the old days, I was beautiful then
I remember the time I knew what happiness was
Let the memory live again.

This second verse has the *same tune* as the first verse. So it's also an 'a' (this is always determined by the tune). So the table now reads:

	Intro	four bars B♭ major, $\frac{12}{8}$ time
a	Verse 1	eight bars
a	Verse 2	eight bars

7 Every street-lamp seems to beat a fatalistic warning
Someone mutters/And a street-lamp gutters
And soon it will be morning

A different bit! A sort of middle. Call it 'b'.

	Intro	four bars B♭ major, $\frac{12}{8}$ time
a	Verse 1	eight bars
a	Verse 2	eight bars
b	Middle	eight bars

8 Daylight, I must wait for the sunrise
I must think of the new life, and I mustn't give in
When the dawn comes tonight will be a memory too
And a new day will begin.

Another 'a'!

	Intro	four bars B♭ major, $\frac{12}{8}$ time
a	Verse 1	eight bars
a	Verse 2	eight bars
b	Middle	eight bars
a	Verse 3	eight bars

9 **You'll find an awful lot of songs in the shape (the musical term is *form*) of 'Memory'. It's called an 'aaba' form.**

10 **Next comes an instrumental break.**
That's a good clue that the song's form ends here, and starts again. In fact in this song there are more words later, but no more tune.

   The instrumental break is another 'a', so label it as such, noting that it has gone into a new key.

Then there's another middle (sung with new words) and a last 'a' section, followed by a four-bar ending similar to the intro.

	Intro	four bars B♭ major, $\frac{12}{8}$ time
a	Verse 1	eight bars
a	Verse 2	eight bars
b	Middle	eight bars
a	Verse 3	eight bars
a	Instrumental	eight bars – F♯ major!
b	Middle	eight bars
a	Verse 4	eight bars – D♭ major!
	Ending	four bars

And there you have it – a complete routine of 'Memory'!

The lead sheet

11 **Make a *lead sheet* using this routine.**
A lead sheet is a piece of written-out music containing the following things (all the info you need to perform the song, as briefly expressed as possible):

The song title
The name of the composer, lyricist and arranger
The tempo and feel of the song
The melody
The words
The chord symbols (*)
The melody of any intro, break or ending

12 **So, the top of your lead sheet should look like this:**

MEMORY

Music by Andrew Lloyd Webber   Arranged by
Text by Trevor Nunn after T. S. Eliot   (put your own name)

13 Now start writing the tune out – but think ahead!
For instance, after you've done the intro, which looks like this:

GENTLY

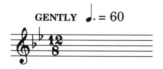

– well, let's look at that intro first. Mark it 'intro' to show that the music here isn't a vocal. The chord symbol (*) B♭ continues in force until cancelled – i.e., for the whole intro. The word GENTLY gives you some idea how to play the song.

14 If you want to fix the tempo exactly, use a metronome speed.
Find the right tempo by experimenting with a metronome and then mark it:

GENTLY ♩. = 60

– i.e., one beat (in this case a dotted crotchet) equals sixty on your metronome. (This means sixty beats per minute.)

15 So, after you've done your intro, note that you've got two 'a' sections together. **Save time by writing repeat signs.**

V.1 Mid - night,   not a sound from the   pave - ment
V.2 Mem - ory,   all a - lone   in the   moon - light

Repeat the B♭ chord symbol, as it's the beginning of a section. Put each bit of a word under its own note, and add hyphens between each bit of word.

Don't get the notes so close together that you can't fit the words in! Resist the temptation to try to get the whole song on to one sheet of manuscript – **spread it out and make it legible.** THIS IS FOR OTHER PEOPLE TO READ!

16 If there are slight differences in notes or rhythm between verses 1 and 2, write in both, putting verse 1's stems up and verse 2's down.

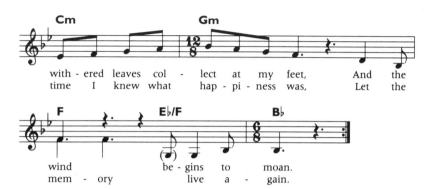

with - ered leaves col - lect at my feet, And the
time I knew what hap - pi - ness was, Let the

wind be - gins to moan.
mem - ory live a - gain.

In the second part of the third bar I used the other method, which is to put any notes that occur in one verse but not in the other, in brackets.

17 Now we're at the middle.

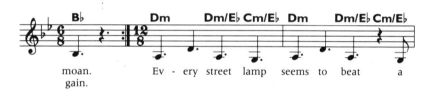

moan. Ev - ery street lamp seems to beat a
gain.

18 When you get to the next 'a' section there's no useful way of repeating back. So you'll have to copy out this 'a' again.

mor - ning. Day - light, I must wait for the sun - rise,

At the end of the middle section I put a double bar-line (both lines thin) to help the reader see that this is a section-ending.

19 Now the instrumental break arrives.

I'm going to cheat now in order to show you more wonders later. On the record the music changes key here. I'm going to carry on in B♭, otherwise I can't demonstrate Dal 𝄋 (see below).

INSTRUMENTAL

20 Use Dal 𝄋 (D. 𝄋 , dal segno) for repeating larger sections.
After the instrumental break, what's left is a 'b' followed by an 'a' section. WE'VE HAD THAT EXACT ORDER BEFORE!
So, at the end of the instrumental break, mark a double bar and:

Dal segno is the Italian for 'from the sign'. It tells the reader to go back in the music and look for a 𝄋.

Plant a 𝄋 back at the middle section!

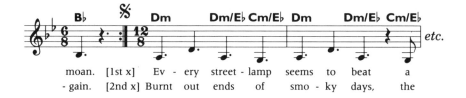

You'll now have to copy the second lot of words underneath the first. Mark them (2nd ×) – × means times, or times, as in multiplication. Silly but effective!

21 Use the ⨁ (coda) sign to re-route the reader to the ending.
(*Al coda* is the Italian for 'to the ending'.)
You don't want the music to reach the instrumental this time, though: you want to go to the ending.

So you plant the coda sign ⨁ after the last bar you can use both times:

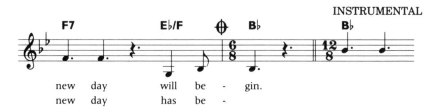

Now write out the ending (coda) after everything you've written so far, if possible leaving a wide space to help the eye.

Note that the tails on the ending melody are all going up in the first bar. This is simply to get them out of the way of the last note of the vocal.

22 If the music is going back to the very beginning, the correct sign is DC (not Dal 𝄌).

DC is short for *da capo*, Italian for 'from the head'. You don't need to put a sign into the beginning of the part. DC al ⊕ is used just like Dal 𝄌 al ⊕.

23 Finally, go through the music adding rehearsal letters.

Rehearsal letters – ⎡A⎤ ⎡B⎤ , etc. – are easy reference points for everybody to use at rehearsal.

'Let's go from letter ⎡B⎤.'

'Let's go from four after ⎡C⎤.'

Rehearsal letters should be copied (at the same places!) into all the players' parts.

Obvious enough, but it's easy to forget them, and it's a real time-waster if you do!

24 So now you have your finished lead sheet:

MEMORY

Music: Andrew Lloyd Webber
Words: T. Nunn, T.S. Eliot

Arranged by
Tony Visconti

sun - rise, I must think of the new life and I must-n't give in. When the
leave me All a-lone with the me - mory of my days in the sun. If you

dawn comes to-night will be a me-mo-ry too, And a new day will be-
touch me you'll un-der-stand what hap-pi-ness is. Look, a new day has be-

-gin.

-gin.

-gun.

INSTRUMENTAL

CODA

rall.

More details

The following things don't occur during 'Memory', but you should know about them.

25 Use slurs to cover several notes which share the same syllable.

26 Use first- and second-time boxes when the ending of a repeated section is slightly different.

Second time through, the player jumps from the end of the third bar straight to the second-time box.

27 In recording situations you can end on a fade-out.

Write a repeat, and 'MECH FADE' after it. (MECH stands for mechanical, i.e., done by a machine, not by the players.)

Tutorial 2: Routining a new arrangement

A singer brings a song to you to be arranged. A band wants a new arrangement of a standard. (A standard is any well-known song.) The first thing to do is plan a routine for the new arrangement.

28 In routining an arrangement of your own you must decide the best SHAPE for the needs of your group.

> What kind of intro, if any?
> How many times through the tune?
> Instrumental breaks?
> Improvised sections?
> What kind of ending?

29 Specialized jazz routining
Things such as head arrangements, open-ended solos and solo backings need separate attention.

Please turn to Chapter 14.

30 Fix on a key, tempo and style for the arrangement.
For a song, consult your singer! (See Chapter 2, **1 – 3**.)

For an instrumental arrangement, choose a good key for your players. All good players can play in any key, but some are more comfortable than others.

> Saxes and brass like (concert pitch) G, C, F, B♭, E♭ and A♭ major, and D, G, C, F, B♭ and E♭ minor.

> Strings don't mind what key you write in, but prefer ♯s to ♭s.

> Guitars like E, A, D, G and C major and minor.

> Keyboards like any of the above keys.

> Drummers are oblivious to the problem!

31 If the tune is on a solo instrument, write in a nice key within the range of that instrument.
Sounds obvious, but it's easy to get this wrong. Your 'easy G major' on the keyboard is E major (four sharps) for an alto sax; and that

ordinary-sounding top G 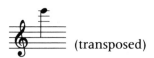 is a high screech for her/him:

(transposed)

Consult your player!

32 Isolate the basic shape (form) of the song or tune.
Play or listen to the song or tune and see what is the shortest shape that gets all the music in with the minimum amount of repetition.

It's like finding the lowest common denominator.

Usually, if it's a song, the whole lyric will have been used once only. (In 'Memory', above, this wasn't so.)

33 Some common shapes to look out for.

aaba   See above.

a b   Verse chorus, verse chorus (common in rap songs and elsewhere).

a1 a2   Tune in two halves, almost the same, only the end of each half different. (You can use first- and second-time boxes, see **25** above.)

a   The same few bars over and over. A twelve-bar blues would come into this category.

34 Having determined the form of your tune, think about how to start the arrangement.

There are only two ways:

    1) With an introduction (intro)

    2) Straight into the tune

Most rock, pop and indy records today have intros, often quite long ones. This has the advantage of establishing a 'feel' (or gradually building one up by adding one instrument to another). It also gives any DJs or announcers something to talk across without blotting out the words of the song.

35 Decide how many times through you'll have the tune played or sung, including instrument breaks.

With 'Memory' (above) it was one and three-quarter times through.

With 'aaba' shapes, this is a usual routine. So is twice through.

With 'a' and 'ab' shapes you will want to go on until the whole lyric (every verse) has been done, plus one or two instrumental breaks, perhaps.

With 'a1', 'a2' you may do the song through once, then have an instrumental break which is an 'a1', then have 'a2' sung. So twice through.

36 Plan any key changes.

If you change key half-way through the song, you won't be able to write a Dal 𝄋 (see **20** above).

That's no reason not to change key if it's right to do so. But it's a great temptation if you're in a hurry!

37 Decide on an ending (if any).

A tune can just finish, or have a special ending (how many bars?), or a fade-out if it's recorded.

38 Jot down a routine based on these decisions.
Do this exactly as described for 'Memory', above.

39 Now plan a lead sheet for the arrangement.
Try to plan the shortest way of getting your intentions on to paper, using repeat signs, first- and second-time boxes, Dal 𝄋 al 𝄌, etc.

40 Write out the lead sheet.
Do this exactly as described in **11–24** above.

41 If you're going to do a full score, you may not need to write out a lead sheet.
You can go straight from the routine to the score, though you will find a lead sheet a great help until you're very experienced.

Tutorial 3: Routining your own tune

42 When you write a tune or song, nine times out of ten the routine will suggest itself.
As you compose it, you hear it in an 'ideal' version, with intro, instrumental breaks, etc. Go with that – it's probably a great idea (because it came without being 'thought out').

Thinking it out is great – always. But ideas which *present themselves* are often even more excellent.

43 As with any other routine, jot down the overall shape (the routine), then do a lead sheet.
It *may* be a good idea to isolate the bare shape of the song, as in **32** above. Or this may not be necessary.

Writing out the routine in 'abac' from (or whatever) will help you make the most efficient lead sheet.

44 If you're going to do a full score, you may not need to write out a lead sheet.
You can go straight from the routine to the score, though you will find a lead sheet a great help until you're very experienced.

45 Don't forget to choose the right key for your composition (see 30 and 31 above).
Remember, the easy key for you to compose in (on your guitar or keyboard) may not suit the singer or player who will end up performing the tune.

Consult! Consult!

Overview

46 The routine

a) Decide on the best shape (form) for the arrangement.
b) Fix on a key, tempo and style.
c) Isolate the basic shape of the tune.
d) Decide on an intro, if any.
e) How many time through the tune?
f) Instrumental breaks?
g) Plan any key changes.
h) Decide on an ending, if any.

Write out a routine based on this, using a, b, c, etc. to label the various sections.

47 The lead sheet

a) Write out the title of the tune and the name(s) of the composer, lyricist and arranger.
b) Use the routine you've made to find the shortest way of getting your arrangement on to paper. See this chapter and Appendix 1 for short cuts.
c) Put in a tempo mark (words and/or metronome speed).
d) Write out the tune
        the words
        the chord symbols (*)
        the melody of any intro, break or ending.
e) Add rehearsal letters.

UNFREE

2 Vocals

Many vocals benefit from echo (delay) and other treatments. See Chapter 9.

There are lead vocals (plus rapping).
There are backing vocals (bvox).
There are a capella vocals (complete arrangements for voices without rhythm section).
For a capella vocals please turn to Chapter 13.

Lead vocals: sung

For how to write out a lead vocal, see the section on the lead sheet (**11–24**) in Chapter 1.

1 Consult your singer about the key.
Each singer has her or his own vocal range and will feel more comfortable singing in certain parts of that range than in others.

For most singers there is a 'best' key for any song. Move the key up or down by even a semitone, and the singer will feel less comfortable.

Put the song in the wrong key for your singer, and you've rendered a good arrangement useless!

Tip: remember that when a singer croons a melody at a first rehearsal or meeting, she or he will probably sing it lower than when belting it out over a band. Singing is about energy, more so than instrumental playing, even drumming. So make your singer really 'give it one' before settling on a key.

2 Chest voice, head voice
In everybody's voice, the low part is good for powerful singing, the high part is shriller and lighter. According to the parts of the body these voices come from, they are called chest voice (power) and head voice (lighter).

In everybody's voice there is a break between chest and head voice. (Actually the two overlap a bit and the overlapping notes can be done in either chest or head.)

Most women's break is at about D

Most men's break is at about F♯

In your arrangement, exploit chest and head voices for stylistic effect.

3 **Consult your singer about tempo, feel, length, etc.**

At the meeting with the singer when you discuss the keys, you will inevitably find yourself talking about other details of the arrangement as well. This is a good thing!

Singers have preferred styles in which to sing (some singers can do several styles; others, equally good – indeed great – can only do one. You wouldn't ask Satchmo to sing an arrangement done for Paul McCartney!).

It is *useless* trying to force on a singer an arrangement which doesn't suit her or his style.

Our voices are built in, not only to our bodies, but to our personalities. My voice is me. If someone sings one way only, *then that's the way they sing.* They may even feel threatened by somebody expecting them to change what is part of their personality.

So, go with, not against, your singer. This way, she or he will sound at their best, and so will your arrangement.

As a wise person once said, it's easier to ride the horse in the direction it's going in.

4 **Give the lead vocal plenty of space. Keep the backing simple. Don't allow accompaniment figures to compete with the lead vocal.**

This is not as obvious as it seems, and I for one have often fallen into the trap of over-arranging the backing.

Let's take an example: any song you like, recorded at his peak (the 1950s), by Frank Sinatra.

I don't care which one you listen to (they crop up a lot on the radio – find an MOR station (middle-of-the-road, light music)).

There's the rhythm section – piano, guitar, bass, drums – swinging along in a great laid-back groove. The saxes and brass put in slinky fills and roof-raising stabs – *where*??

In the gaps in the vocals! While Sinatra is taking breaths. Under the long held notes. Anywhere except where it would compete with Ol' Blue-eyes.

Now listen to any great record in your own favourite style, be it hip-hop or folk.

Same thing, huh?

The good arrangers know this!

5 Does your singer have a microphone?
Against modern instruments, and particularly drums, the unamplified human voice has big problems. They can be overcome, but you have to arrange with superhuman care and tact!

Make the rhythm section play quiet! Keep reminding them, they don't like doing it.

Keep the arranged texture as thin as possible. Less instruments mean less competition.

Give the lead vocal even more space.

A single saxophone or trumpet will drown an unamplified voice.

Try to keep the accompaniment out of the pitch-area of the voice. If the singer is, say, a man whose range is

– don't write accompanying instruments in that range. You can't avoid this, of course, in the rhythm section – but even there keep it thin!

Lead Vocals: rap

6 Rap is rhythmic talking over a band.

7 All the tips I've given for sung lead vocals (1–5 above) apply just as much to rapping – especially the ones about space and balance.
Consult your rapper!

8 Not every singer can rap!
You'd be surprised (and disappointed) how many good singers are not remotely good at rap. It's almost a different instrument.

They say that music is handled by the right side of the human brain, words by the left side. Some people are talented on one side and not on the other (a tone-deaf actor, for example, has her or his left brain more developed than the right). Perhaps this is why some good singers can't rap.

Consult your singer before writing rap!

9 Write rap like sung vocals (see the section on the lead sheet (11–24) in Chapter 1), but use crosses instead of note-heads.

Accents and stresses can be used to suggest interpretation.

10 You can make the crosses go up and down to suggest rough pitch differences.

Backing vocals (bvox)

Bvox is pronounced 'Beevox'.
Popular music has always had backing vocals:
>   The choir doubling the lead vocal in a country and western song
>   The choir behind Bing Crosby in 'White Christmas'
>   The Supremes behind Diana Ross
>   The Beatles doing their own bvox countermelodies
>   Ladysmith Black Mambazo behind Paul Simon

Historically there are various roots for bvox.
>   The chorus in operetta and musicals
>   Gospel singing
>   Singalong
>   A capella, barber-shop
>   Swing groups such as the Andrews Sisters

11 For some stupid reason, in pop arranging bvox singers are always referred to as 'girls' and 'boys', even when they're middle-aged!
There are also children's voices: write as for 'girls' below, but remember that children's voices are less powerful.

12 These are the ranges of the voices if you want an unforced, easy sound.

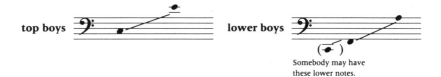

top boys   lower boys

(○)
Somebody may have
these lower notes.

13 If you want something more powerful, say in a gospel or alternatively a 'classical' style, you can extend the ranges upwards:

But note, if you write up there, the velvet will disappear.

top girls   lower girls   top boys   lower boys

Chorus backing

14 Depending on the number of singers available, you can write for chorus in four, five or six parts.

girls

boys

You can get away with two voices per part, but to sound really 'choral' you need at least three. Three on the top girls' line and two each underneath is a reasonable compromise.

15 If the music is simple, write out the choral parts on two staves, girls in the upper, boys in the lower.

girls

CHORUS   Sing   some - thing   sin - ful.

boys

Put the words in the space between the staves.

16 If the whole choir is unison, still use two staves.

CHOIR

17 If the music is too complex to put on two staves, give each line its own stave:

Note that the top boys (the tenors), if they have their own line, like to use a special clef, a treble clef with a small 8 attached to the bottom. This sounds an octave below the true treble clef.

The words here are scat (see **23** below).

18 You may have just female or just male voices.

Write on two staves:

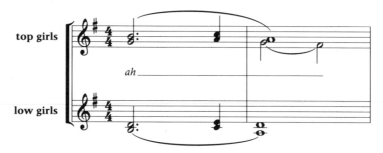

19 With a choir, you don't *have* to give the singers anywhere to breathe!

If there are three persons on each part, they can breathe unobtrusively in different places.

20 Traditionally, choir bvox is written simple.

If you choose to write complicated, fair enough. You should expect to need lots of rehearsal, though. (Choral singers aren't always the best sight-readers. No intended libel on King's College!)

Three girls, three boys (four is also good)

21 Write on one stave if at all feasible.

22 You can use unison as well as harmonies.

23 Bvox singers often do 'hip' nonsense words, called 'scat'.

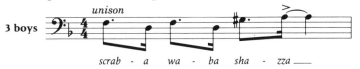

Scat often looks embarrassing on the page, but sounds better than it looks! For a supreme use of scat (albeit in lead vocals), listen to the work of Ella Fitzgerald.

24 Wordless passages are effective.

25 Remember to write in places for the singers to breathe.
If in doubt whether a phrase you've written is too long for one breath, sing it yourself, quite loud. If you can do it, the singers should be able to.

Lead singer as bvox

26 You can of course only do this in the recording studio.
On many pop records you'll hear bvox which are the lead singer's voice, multitracked. It gives a very personal sound to the song.
    And it's cheap.
    Write just like any other bvox.

Do-it-themselves bvox

27 It can be great fun to work out the bvox at the rehearsal, in collaboration with the singers.
So it won't be all your own work. So what? It'll be all the fresher for that! And you'll get the credit in the end, anyway!

3 The Rhythm Section

Arranging for rhythm section

Having routined your song, you know where the melody/lead vocals will go, and where any intros, breaks or endings will be.

The next thing to do is to fix the rhythm parts.

1 **By rhythm section we mean all or any of the following instruments:**

> **Drums**
> **Percussion**
> **Bass**
> **Guitars**
> **Keyboards**

In other words, the rhythm section is the basic accompanying unit of any arrangement. You could do the whole song just with the rhythm section and a lead instrument/vocal. If you use a member of the rhythm section for your lead, that's ALL you need.

Backing vocals (*), brass (*), saxes (*), strings (*), solo instruments – these are all extras, luxuries to use if you have them.

You can't DO an arrangement without a rhythm section (**except an a capella (*) arrangement**).

2 **Decide whether or not to make a score (*) of your arrangement (see Chapter 15 for the score). If not, make a lead sheet (*) and work from that.**
The advantage of a score is that you have a complete written account of your arrangement, a kind of bible you can refer to if there are any queries – and there will be!

The disadvantage is, a score takes a very long time to write out, after which you'll still have the instrumental parts to copy out.

If the arrangement and routine is simple, and you think you can keep it in your head easily, then do a lead sheet (*).

There are lots of short cuts in score-writing to save you time. See Appendix 1.

3 Working from the lead sheet or score, decide exactly where you want each instrument to play.
You don't want to have everybody pounding away all through the song.

If you've got a percussion player, have the drummer drop out for eight bars occasionally.

If you've got backing vocals, they can sustain the beat and the harmonies a capella (*) for a while.

Intros and endings are sometimes more effective with a single instrument, or a gradual building of instruments.

You can alter the **texture** of the arrangement by getting various instruments (guitar, keyboard, bass, drums, percussion) to drop out for a while.

Think of your rhythm section as a long strip of carpet along which the music walks. You can have the carpet all the same width and colour, or you can have it change.

Both methods work.

4 Copy out parts for each rhythm section instrument.
IMPORTANT!

5 Make sure that each part is laid out exactly the same.
It wastes enormous amounts of rehearsal time if the guitar part has a D 𝄋 (*) where the drum part doesn't.

Use rehearsal letters or numbers, and make sure they are exactly the same on all parts.

6 If you've done a repeat or a D 𝄋 (*) and you suddenly realize you want something different (a guitar solo, say) the second time, all is not lost!

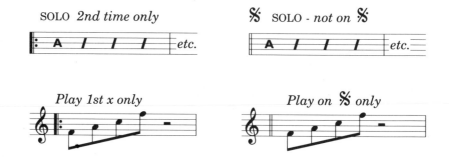

7   **You may find that one part (photocopied) will do for more than one instrument.**
    If the arrangement is very simple, just a chord chart, say, then it will do for bass, guitar and keyboards.

(photocopied)

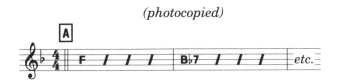

8   **The lead sheet (photocopied) may be all the rhythm section needs for a part.**
    Or you may have to give the drums and percussion their own parts.
       But if the arrangement gets at all complicated, your musicians will appreciate (and will grumble if they don't get!) individual parts.

9   **For how to write each part, see the chapters for the instruments you're using.**

Sequencing (see also Chapter 9, **15–22**)

If you're working with synthesized rhythm and a sequencer, the following tips may be useful.

10   **Get a drum pattern first.**
    Work on a repeated eight-bar loop and get that to your liking.

11   **Settle on a bass-drum pattern, then add snare, hi-hat and percussion.**

12   **When you're happy with that, think about toms, crash cymbals and other occasional events.**
    A tom-fill will come at an important turning-point in the song – generally at the end of an eight-bar section.

13   **Add bass to the drums, making a tight pattern.**
    See 'Bass and drums' in Chapter 4.

14   **Having got your eight-bar loop right, sequence your whole arrangement.**
    Add your synth keyboards and any other instruments you want to use.

15 Always be prepared to go back and change something if it doesn't work when you add more instruments.

It's just like cooking – you may find you've added too much pepper and garlic – but with sequencing (unlike cooking) you can remove the offending ingredient at any stage!

Recording

16 If you have access to recording equipment, the rhythm section is the first thing to lay down.

You can even have the luxury of doing arrangement in two parts:

1) Routine and record the rhythm section – this is called the **rhythm track** (even though it may take up several tracks on a multitrack tape-recorder).

2) Put your rhythm track, roughly mixed, on to a cassette, take it away and decide at your leisure what extra arranging needs to be done (e.g. adding bvox (*), brass (*), strings (*), etc., etc.).

17 The lead vocal (or lead instrument) is always the last thing you record.

And when you've done it, you may well find that there are more adjustments to make to the backing. That's life!

DRUMS   UNFREE

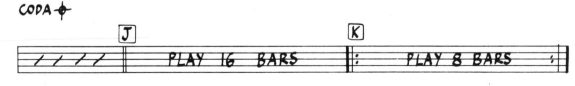

4 Drums

'A drummer can do what a drummer can do.'

The main message of this chapter is contained in the above quote: drummers, more than any other instrumentalists, have their own licks, their own strengths (and weaknesses) – their own individual style. To ask a drummer to play in a style other than her or his own can be to court disaster.

Some players are more flexible than others. Listen to your player and judge for yourself. *All* players prefer to play in their own style.

The kit

1 Bass drum

The bass drum is played with a foot-pedal. It makes a loud, dull thump.

Notate:

Throughout the history of popular music the bass drum has been at the centre of the time-keeping of all bands. Take marching bands, for example, whether military, high-school, pipe or New Orleans. The players march and play in time with the bass drum (here a single drum carried strapped to the chest and played with a padded stick). The bass drum player starts the music with a signal which gives the tempo and beats it in, and ends it with another which gives no doubt where to stop:

So, right up to the present day, the bass drum in a drum kit is the 'rock' around which the player builds her or his pattern.

This means that the bass drum plays on the first beat of most bars in most arrangements (first and third in $\frac{4}{4}$ time). In some music, e.g. reggae, this is deliberately *not* done occasionally. You can ask your player to experiment – it seems to 'throw the music off' in an interesting way.

2 Snare drum

The snare drum is played with either drum-sticks or wire brushes. Hard rhythms are done with sticks, while the brushes make a softer, swishy sound, and can play long notes. The only way to do a long note with the sticks is to do a roll.

Notate:

3 Hi-hat cymbals

The hi-hat is a stack of two medium–small cymbals which can be clashed together using a foot-pedal, or played with drum-sticks or wire brushes.

I use crosses instead of note-heads for hi-hat: it makes it easier for the drummer to distinguish from the other drums. But it's a matter of taste.

Notate:

The cross through the stems of various notes indicates 'Play this note with the pedal'.

A remarkable range of subtle effects can be got out of the hi-hat, many of them by striking the top cymbal with sticks or brushes while closing or half-closing the pedal. To my knowledge, no system of notating these subtleties has ever been accepted as standard.

Therefore, the best way of writing for the hi-hat as a separate instrument is to write a few beats of the sort of rhythm you want, and then 'continue sim.' (i.e., similar):

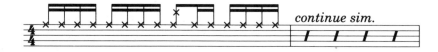

4 Tom-toms (or just toms)

The tom-toms are the drums you hear blobling around in a 'drum fill' at the end of an eight-bar section.

Toms are resonant drums, often with no bottom skin. There are two or three toms of different sizes in most drum kits; sometimes only one, occasionally as many as six or seven. The different sizes give different pitches (the larger the drum, the higher the pitch). Toms are usually played with sticks.

Notate:

5 Cymbals

Most drum kits have two or three stand cymbals attached. The most usual kinds are:

Splash cymbal	A small cymbal for accenting
Crash cymbal	Larger, for more powerful accents
Ride cymbal	For keeping a steady beat
Chinese cymbal	A thick sound used as a heavier crash or ride

The cymbals are played with either drum sticks or wire brushes. Hard rhythms are done with the sticks, while the brushes make a softer, swishy sound, and can play long notes.

There are two ways to do a long note with the sticks: 1) a roll; 2) scrape a stick across the surface of the cymbal – you get a sort of screech.

Notate:

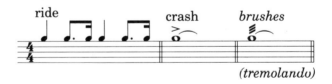

(tremolando)

As you see above, the player will normally use sticks unless you mark 'brushes'.

6 'Toys'

Some drummers carry additional instruments, collectively known as toys, with their kit.

Skulls	Hollow wooden spheres in various sizes
Woodblock	A single hollow wooden box
Klaxon	An old-fashioned motor horn
Maraca(s),	These rattle when shaken.

As you can see, these instruments overlap with Latin-American percussion (*) – some drummers may carry LA instruments as well. Those LA percussion instruments which can be hand-held are also often referred to as 'toys'.

Notate:

The drum part

7 If in doubt what to write, this will always serve:
(as long as you want to write in $\frac{4}{4}$)

(Snare drum stems can go up or down for convenience)

8 Drum parts don't use a clef, just a time signature.

9 To write a drum part, simply add together all the instruments on one stave.

Insert rests *only* where the rhythm would otherwise not be obvious.

10 The drummer will play more than you write.
Unless you specifically mark to the contrary, a drummer will assume that this –

– means 'play a pattern based on this idea'. She or he will fill out your suggestion to make a total drum sound. **THIS IS AN AMAZING ADVANTAGE!** It means that 1) you don't have to spend hours notating a detailed drum part, and 2) the drummer doesn't have to spend hours deciphering it. You could never write as idiomatically as your drummer plays, anyway.

11 Indicate in words the feel you want.

Then suggest by a *simplified* notation the kind of thing you want.

12 Having indicated the feel, continue *similar* with slashes for each beat.

Give the feel in words, then in one or two bars' simplified notation, then as follows:

13 If you want a drum fill, write the word 'fill' where you want it.

You can specify a light or heavy fill.

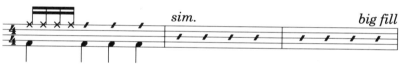

14 If you want the drummer to continue in the same way for a number of bars, say so in words.

If you are using rehearsal letters (*) in your arrangement, write in the number of bars until the next letter, mark the letter, and carry on.

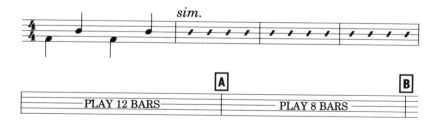

That way, when the conductor or bandleader says, 'We'll go from letter B', the drummer will know where to start!

15 Make your drum part as simple as possible!

I know I'm hammering this, but truly I have found that the more I write in a drum part, the more trouble I get with the drummer.

Surprisingly sparse instructions will get the required sound *better* than a cluttered part. Believe me.

Double-time feel

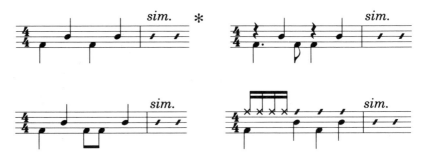

16 The following are some usual ways of indicating a drum pattern:

Don't forget, the drummer will play *more* than this; this is just short-hand.

Four of the most common patterns in rock:

Jazz beat:

Dotted feel

*   This is a great all-purpose notation for anything in $\frac{4}{4}$. If in any doubt, use it and write the feel you want in words. Here's the same idea for $\frac{3}{4}$:

Note that the 'jazz triplet' is always notated ♩. ♪ . You could also write in words 'dotted feel', which means the same thing. Even when you've written this you must still dot your quavers in the part.

Bass (*) and drums

The most important relationship within the rhythm section is that between the drummer and bass player.

17 Make sure you write bass and drum parts that interlock nicely.
The less specific and simpler you write (here I go again) for both bass and drums, the better the chance that the players will find something that fits well together.

It's *always* better to discuss with your players what you want, and leave it to them to come up with something – which you can then modify.

See also Chapter 5, section 3.

Synth drums

Many people these days have synthesized drums, either as an add-on to their synth or organ, or as a separate unit. The simpler machines give you pre-programmed rhythms, and they sound about as good as you'd expect. The more complex drum synths let you program your own patterns, then link several patterns together into a tailor-made drum sequence for your whole song. These can sound (different from but) as good as real drums.

18 Spend a day 'learning' your drum machine.
You can't just sit down and *play* a drum kit without practice, and similarly you can't just play a drum machine. Mind you, it won't take you as long to learn as the real drums, because

1) you can keep doing the same four bars (or one bar if you're a real beginner) over and over until you get them right, then 'save' them to memory while you perfect the next four!
2) there is a funky button on a drum machine called 'Quantize', which automatically corrects your unhip time and turns it into wonderful drumming!

So, to get the best out of your machine, play with it for some hours before using it for real. Work out three or four different patterns – none of them the one you will want to use in your arrangement. Then when you do come to do your real drum sequence it will be six times as good as it would otherwise have been.

19 Use your imagination to create the right drum pattern for your arrangement.

Don't over-arrange the drum machine: there won't be any room left in the listener's ears for the music.

What I do when sequencing a track with synths and drums is to make the drums simple enough – just bass drum and snare, say – to provide the basic pulse and feel. Then I do the rest of the track – bass, synths, etc. Then I go back to the synth drums and add anything extra that's needed, hi-hat throughout perhaps, a toms fill here, some crash cymbal there. It's amazing how little I find I need to add.

Some arrangers do it from the other end, making a complex bass-and-drums sequence first and adding the rest on top. This gives a much more rhythm-heavy feel, which I don't usually choose but which you may like. Try both ways and choose for yourself.

20 You can do things on a drum machine that no drummer would have the technique to do.

No drummer has enough arms to do a snare drum roll, a toms fill and hit two cymbals all at once. But you can do that easily on a drum machine.

So you should start your arrangement with a clear idea: are you reproducing only what a real drummer could play, or is the sky the limit? Both ways of working are valid. I just want you to choose one or the other.

21 If you need to write out a part for a drum machine, make it look exactly like an ordinary drum part.

UNFREE

5 Bass

There are three main instruments for playing a bassline: bass guitar, synth bass and string bass (double bass).

Bass guitar: fretted

1 **Write the part in chord symbols (*) or notes, or a mixture of both.**

2 **Notes are written in the bass clef and sound an octave below:**

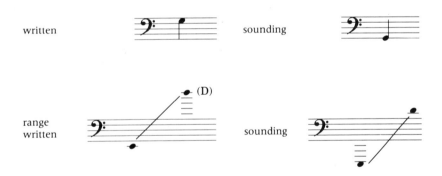

The player could tune his bottom string down below E, but it's rarely done. The tone deteriorates, and the playing of licks which include notes on the bottom string becomes tricky.

Some basses have fretboards that go higher than top D (e.g. Aria). Consult your player.

For really high passages, all those ledger-lines are hard to read, so an alternative is to write the music an octave down, marking the part to be played an octave higher:

difficult to read

easier to read

You *could* use the treble clef for high passages, but not all (actually not *many*) bass-players read it.

Bass guitar style

3 When writing for bass guitar, leave as much as possible to the player – so use mostly chord symbols.
If you are rehearsing with the players, you have the opportunity to discuss the basic rhythm feel you are aiming for. The key people in this discussion are the bassist and the drummer. Take their advice to a certain extent – if you force them to play licks they're uncomfortable with they'll sound like a bad rhythm section. On the other hand, be positive as to what you want, and don't let them railroad you into licks you don't think suitable. That way you'll all end up hating each other!

4 At the start of the part suggest a style in words and notes.
If you are positive you know what you want from the rhythm section, give it to them in writing (and be prepared to alter it!). If you are delivering an arrangement to someone else's band a discussion may not be possible, so you'll have to give them a clear idea *on the part* as to what you intend.

You can write instructions in words, such as funky, mellow, reggae, disco, jazz 4 (walking bass), etc. It is a good idea, however, to supplement these words with a bar or two of actual notes suggesting a pattern the player should use – because words (like funky) mean different things to different players.

Reggae

The word 'sim' over the third bar (Italian *simile*) means 'Carry on in the same style'.

Special fx

5 Harmonics: your player will demonstrate what's available.
Harmonics are very individual to particular players, so leave her or
him to do them unless you're very sure you know what you want,
and that it's possible on the instrument.

Writing down harmonics is a can of worms. Basically you write a
small circle over the note ![notation] – but unfortunately this notation is ambiguous. It might mean 'Play a harmonic which sounds a
C' but it might also mean 'Finger a C and play the harmonic on that
fret' – which unhappily produces a G. Writers and players have never
sorted this idiocy out between themselves, mostly because harmonics
are more often improvised than written. Consult your player!

6 Slap bass; two-hand slap: don't attempt to write this out!
If you want to, write 'slap bass' or 'two-hand slap' in words and give
chord symbols.

7 Pedals and boxes: check what your player owns.
Many fx boxes work well with bass. I can't predict which ones will
turn you (or your bass players) on, but I like compressors and enve-
lope followers. So experiment. DON'T WRITE FOR AN EFFECT IF
YOU HAVEN'T HEARD IT! It probably won't sound how you imagined,
and it may not even work. You could look a fool.

8 Fretted basses don't sustain all that long.

9 A bass player's sound is her or his own.
A bass player may be wiling to change her or his sound (e.g. more highs
for slap, more lows for reggae), but remember that every player's
sound is her or his trademark, personal fingerprint. Respect that.

Bass guitar: fretless

**10 Everything in the section on fretted bass applies equally to
fretless, and –**

11 Fretless basses sustain magnificently.

12 Fretless style tends more to swoops and slides.

Write a slide as follows

13 On a fretless you can do a slide on a harmonic.

14 You can't do slap bass on a fretless.

15 Different fx boxes work well on a fretless.
Especially ones linked to a long sustain, such as chorus, phase and distort. Again, these are purely subjective judgements. Experiment! Consult your player!

Synth bass

16 Bass guitar and synth bass are interchangeable. BUT THEY ARE NOT THE SAME.
The message is, if you have a synth bass to write for, don't try to make it a substitute bass guitar. It has a different style.
Different, how?
The differences all stem from the mechanics of the two instruments.
Because the bass guitar has four strings on a fingerboard, certain melodic shapes come naturally to the player's hand. Also certain techniques such as 'hammering down', sliding, accenting, slapping, stopping the sound, etc. All these techniques are basically guitar players' tricks, for a bass guitar is first and foremost a guitar.
The synth player, on the other hand, thinks in keyboard terms. Her or his tricks include rapid finger-passages, wide leaps, touch variation, use of the pitch-bend and mod wheels (*) and a variety of different sounds, including ones which change as they sustain. All this leads to a bassline which is exciting in a totally different way from the excitement of a bass guitar line.

17 Write the part in chord symbols (*) or notes, or a mixture of both.

18 Write a synth bass part on one stave, mostly within the bass clef.

The player will probably make it come out an octave lower. If the part goes below bottom C, she or he can't, as that's the bottom note on most synths.
If the part goes high, use the treble clef.

19 The essence of synth bass is the sound, which is infinitely changeable.
The first thing to do when writing for synth bass is to decide on a sound. You can get anything, from a totally characterless, almost

subliminal drone, through mellow ballad and punchy funk, to a really harsh, assertive timbre for mechanistic pieces.

20 **Decide roughly what sound you want, describe it in words, consult your player.**
Stay open as to the exact sound you want until you hear the player's ideas. She or he may have good ones, and the experience to know what works!

21 **Remember, a sound appears duller when you hear it inside the music.**
Once the rest of the band start to play, the bass sound will appear duller than it does solo. So make it quite a lot brighter (add highs) than you think ideal when listening to it on its own.

22 **When writing for synth bass, leave as much as possible to the player – so mostly use chord symbols.**
See **3** above.

23 **At the start of the part suggest a style in words and notes.**
See **4** above. For synth bass you will be specifying a) sound and b) style.

Bass guitar or synth bass?

24 **If you're lucky enough to have the choice, choose either bass guitar or synth bass for its strengths and suitability to your arrangement.**
What strengths?
   Again, this is only my opinion. I'd choose a synth bass if I wanted extreme agility; or a rabble-rousing, stirring sound; or very low notes, outside the bass guitar's range; or a very low-profile sound which didn't draw attention to itself, with long, slow notes.
   I'd choose a bass guitar to play a lick repeated over and over (it sounds just that bit more 'human'); for a slow, lyrical number with a lyrical, melodic bassline; for a bassline that is mainly a pulse, interlocking with the drums; obviously for a slap bass number or anything that calls stylistically for bass guitar; or if the group had no other synths playing.

25 **Some synths, especially the samplers, will do extremely life-like bass guitar sounds.**
Here you have two choices, to play it like a synth or like a guitar. In the second case you should not do anything a bass guitar can't do (i.e., don't go below and E and don't play licks which, although easy on a keyboard, would be impossible on a fretboard).

Basic bass licks

26 It is much preferable for you to learn about bass licks by listening to your favourite bands!

I have added this section most reluctantly. If you don't know any good bass licks, listen to your favourite tracks and work out what the bassline is. This will do you more good than reading ten books. Anything I suggest will make your arrangement sound stolid and dull; not because I can't write bass licks but because I can't write *your* bass licks. It is so much better for you (in consultation with your bass player) to come up with your own licks, that I *almost* refuse to show you any. Almost.

27 The most important thing about a bass lick is that it must inter-lock with the drum pattern – especially the bass drum (*).

Good players usually do this naturally, but even they can come unstuck, especially if you, the arranger, write them something naff. Always, where possible, discuss. Where discussion is impossible, leave the written part as open as you can.

And *keep it simple*. (Or not, but make the choice.)

String bass (For string bass in a string section, see Chapter 11)

Use of the string bass is increasing again after a period of neglect. Its main areas of use are jazz, Latin/salsa and '50s-style rock. In all these areas you can use bass guitar or synth bass instead, but to purist fogeys such as myself the string bass is authentic and preferable.

28 Write the part in chord symbols (*) or notes, or a mixture of both.

String bass players prefer following chord symbols.

29 Notes are written in the bass clef and sound an octave below (identical with the bass guitar).

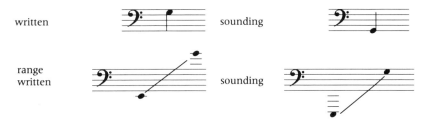

Some players have an extra-long bottom string and can play down to C. Consult your player!

Some virtuoso bassists can play with great agility very high (at least an octave higher than the top G marked above), but these players are a small minority. Even among good professional bassists most players are uncomfortable above G. Consult your player!

If you do write passages including notes above C use either the 8va . . . . notation or the treble clef.

The above passage is relatively easy on the string bass because the high notes can be played as harmonics (the small circles over the notes indicate a harmonic). Put it in *any* other key and it becomes virtually impossible.

String bass style

30 At the start of the part suggest a style in words and notes.

The word '*sim*' over the third bar means 'Carry on in the same style'.

31 The three great traditions in string bass style are two-in-a-bar, walking and Latin-American.

The string bass when amplified can play rock'n'roll, and a very elastic, loose-limbed sound it makes, pokey with a roar at the bottom end. But that is not the style most people think of string bass for.

'50s rock uses broken chords with an added sixth, jazz lines snake about melodically, using scales with added semitones and leaps.

There are many classic Latin bass licks, all quite strictly adhered-to by the music's purists: mambo, tango, pasa doble, bolero, etc. – each has its own distinctive rhythm. As usual with basslines, they interlock in an important way with the percussion patterns.

32 The fourth great tradition in string bass style is free jazz.
In free jazz the player does not play licks or lines but a freely improvised series of rhythmic/melodic patterns, sometimes only loosely related to tempo or harmony. This style is very creative and personal, and any player you meet will either do it or not. By definition you can't write free jazz down, nor can you give the player verbal directions as to what you want, except very vaguely ('busy', 'spare', 'lyrical', 'angry', etc.). Good exponents of the style can do it around a tempo and chord sequence (e.g. Scott LaFaro on the early Bill Evans Trio records) or completely 'outside' time and chords (listen to John Coltrane's later records).

SYNTH.

UNFREE

6 Keyboards

The two main types of keyboard instrument in use today are **synths** (a term I use to mean any synthesizer, sampler or electronic keyboard) and **piano.** Next most common is the electric **organ.** Then there is a group containing electronic or electric pianos, clavinets, electric harpsichords, etc.: this group is tending to die out because you can do the same sounds on a synth. I shall mention them in the synth section where appropriate.

Synths

1 **Write the part in chord symbols (*) or notes, or a mixture of both.**

2 **Use a double stave:**

range

most of the small battery-operated keyboards have this range: on a larger instrument you can go an octave higher *and* lower

Basic technical info

3 **Synths get their sounds in various ways:**

a) **Presets.** All synths have these, usually in the form of buttons or displays with named sounds you can call up. If you know your player's synth you can ask her or him for a particular sound.

b) **Synthesis.** On the larger 'synthesizer'-type synths the player can create her or his own sounds, and make changes to the presets. You could ask her or him to make you a custom sound. Two snags: this takes a lot of time; and your imagined sound may not be possible – the sky's *not* the limit even on instruments only the stars can afford; consult your player!

c) **Sampling.** On a sampler you can feed in any sound – your own voice, a door slam, a recording of a drum, guitar, full orchestra, *anything* – and play it back on the keyboard at any pitch. This gives you a much wider range of sounds to play with, and the sounds can be less 'synthy' too. (See also Chapter 9, **8–14**.)

4 Many synths have other functions you should know about:

a) All but the smallest ones have a **sustain pedal** like a piano.

b) A **pitch-bend wheel** lets you slide and glide around. NB, you need to stop playing with one hand to operate this. When you let go it always returns to the note you started with.

c) A **mod wheel** lets you add vibrato to any sound. You can either operate it with one hand, changing the vibrato as you play, or preset it and play with both hands.

d) **MIDI** is a system to let the player control and/or play several synths at once from just one keyboard: so one player can produce a combination of sounds. This is too complex to go into here, but stunning effects are possible: consult your player!

e) Many synth players also use a **sequencer.** This is like a drum machine in that it automatically plays back music you've programmed into it – but not just drums! You can program a whole song, synth drums, synth bass and keyboards, and use it as a backing track to sing or play to. (See also Chapter 9, **15–22**.)

The sounds of a synth

NB Don't let your imagination be fooled by the name a manufacturer gives a sound. It may be a naff 'trumpet', but it may sound great for some other use. Listen to the sound, not the name.

5 Specify the kind of synth sound you want.

There are three ways of describing a synth sound you'd like to hear:

a) Name the sound if it has a name – synth bass, flute, strings, etc.

b) Name the nearest thing – brassy, sax-like, choir-ish, etc.

c) Use metaphors – warm/cold, brite/dull, hard/soft, sweet/acid, etc.

6 'Electric keyboard' sounds

Common sound-names: piano, grand piano, electric piano, digital electric piano, honky-tonk, clavinet, Rhodes.

7 'Synth'

Common sound-names: lead synth, fantasy, sawtooth, moonlight, warm pad, metal hall, theme, overdrive; the names try to suggest what the sound will be like, usually with little success.

8 Organ (see 'Electric organ' at the end of this chapter)

9 fx

Synths can make the most wonderful (non-strictly musical) noises. The ones you hear on video games are puny, limited examples of this. The odd zap, thunderclap or swish can be very effective (fx-ive!) once or twice in the right song. But just once or twice, OK?

10 Sampled sounds

The people who sell samplers also give you pre-recorded instrumental sounds to play on them (usually stored on disk). Many of these are so lifelike you could get into trouble with other musicians for using them (really!)

Most of the sounds below come in two versions: sampled (lifelike) and synthesized (more obviously synthy) (this is an over-simplification but useful to think about). Both types have their uses: for instance, synth brass is often more appropriate than real (or lifelike sampled) brass.

11 Bass (see also 'Synth bass' in Chapter 5)

Common sound-names: elec bass, syn bass, acou bass, slap bass, funk bass, slide bass; usually quite good guides to the sound.

12 Drums and percussion (see also 'Synth drums' in Chapter 4 and 'Synth percussion' in Chapter 8)

Many synths now have a full range of drum sounds, either preset in a drum machine function or programmable.

13 Brass (see also 'Synth brass and reeds', in Chapter 10)

Common sound-names: synbrass, velo-brass, horn lead, brass section.

14 Strings (see also 'Synth strings' in Chapter 11)

Common sound-names: strings, string section, etc.

15 Flutes (see also Chapter 10, **43**)

Common sound-names: flutes, blowpipe, calliope, pan pipes, piccolo, whistle.

16 Guitar

Synth guitar sounds have a long way to go before they will begin to sound authentic. This is mostly because of the very different playing methods of guitars and synths. How you actually hold an instrument, and what you do to play it, naturally affects the way it sounds very deeply.

However, if you don't have a real guitar you can give quite a good impression of one (acoustic or electric) on some synths. That's if you truly must have a guitar sound.

17 Backing vocals (see also 'Backing vocals (bvox)' in Chapter 2)
On a sampler you can (with care) get a nice 'choir' effect. Of course
it will only sing 'Ah' or whatever you program in, not lyrics (OK, you
can get it to go 'Yeah!' or 'Ow!' over and over).

Uses for synths

18 Synth as a rhythm-section keyboard
(This also applies to electronic/electric pianos of all kinds.)

In this function the more usual sounds would be the keyboard-like
ones: piano, digital electric piano, clavinet, etc. But experiment with
sounds you might not expect – brassy or fluty (and other) sounds in
the rhythm section give the song a completely new flavour.

It's just about impossible to give any list of **basic licks** in this
chapter, because every player has her or his own style.

In general it's better to give chord symbols (*) plus a verbal indi-
cation of what you want – funky, simple ballad, jazz-funk, heavy metal,
reggae. . . . If there is a *particular shape* you *must* have the synth play,
then write it out:

tempo : **funky**   *sound* : **hard synth**

jazz-funk

tempo : **medium**   *sound* : **elec. piano**

rock ballad

tempo : **imposing**   *sound* : **brass**

open fifths

19 Synth as a solo sound

Instead of a guitar break or a sax break you have a synth break. Actual 'synth' sounds are the usual thing here (and there is a wide variety of sounds to choose from on most instruments).

tempo : **brite** *sound* : **lead synth.**

Or you can try unlikely sounds – the upper end of a bass sound, for instance, sometimes has an unexpected timbre.

Or you can use sampled sounds to impersonate some other instrument; but beware – a sound must be *very* lifelike not to be unintentionally comic.

20 Synth as harmony filler (see also 'Synth strings' in Chapter 11, and 'Backing vocals' ('bvox') in Chapter 2)

The synth is used in the same way you would use strings or a choir going 'Ah'. The best sounds for this are the softest-grained ones, with a gradual attack (i.e., no hard start to the note) and lots of chorusing (like several instruments playing at once). After all, it's only there as padding, as a velvet background, not to be noticed.

tempo : **slow** *sound* : **strings**

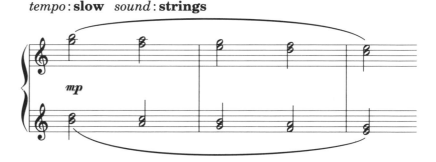

21 Synth as stab and shout merchant (see also 'Synth brass and reeds' in Chapter 10)

In other words, it takes the function of a brass section. The obvious sounds to use are either synth brass (or a brassy synth sound, get the difference?) or sampled brass. But you could look for an unconventional alternative. The sound would have to be bright (if not harsh) with a hard attack.

tempo: **brite** *sound*: **brass**

22 Synth as melodic riff

(This also applies to clavinets and other spiky-sounding instruments: any Wurlitzer pianos left out there?)

Here the synth is used like a rhythm guitar which is picking a repeated pattern. Best sounds are the sharp-edged, short ones such as clavinet, short guitar or a short synth sound.

tempo: **brite** *sound*: **clavinet**

23 Synth as bass, drums, flutes, guitar, bvox, sound fx

See the relevant paragraphs (**11, 12, 15, 16, 17** and **9**) above, and the chapters on the real instruments.

24 Synth as chameleon/instrument impersonator

If you want a particular instrumental sound but don't know a player, the sampler can be the answer. Careful, though, of upsetting other players – and of doing a bad impersonation!

Piano

25 Write the part in chord symbol (*) or notes, or a mixture of both.

26 Use a double stave:

since everyone knows what a piano sounds like, I won't waste space telling you

range

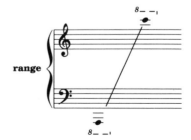

27 Use mostly chord symbols (*)

This lets the player do her or his own thing. Especially if she or he is a keyboard player and you're not, you'll get better results this way.

28 If there is a *particular shape* you *must* have the piano play, write it out:

But there are *so many* **basic licks** on piano, and they are so personal to each player, that it is impossible even to scratch the surface here, and wrong to try – much better to tell you to *consult your player*.

29 Don't over-arrange: sometimes use the piano completely on its own.

It's very effective (you hear it on lots of records) to have the intro to the song on unaccompanied solo piano.

And there are any number of other places within an arrangement where this can be a stunning stroke of the arranger's art – like a sudden cut in the texture to solo piano; or a gradual wind-down to finish the track; use your imagination and do the unexpected!

Electric organ

The electric organ came into pop music by way of the gospel singers. At first sight a most unlikely instrument for swingin' or groovin', the gospel players got (and continue to get) the most extraordinary, funky sounds out of it. By the 1950s the organ had moved in on the jazz scene with the 'soul' music of Jimmy Smith and others. By 1970 it had invaded the rock world led by Georgie Fame and Keith Emmerson. Perhaps slightly eclipsed today by the synthesizer (which can make exactly the same sounds, but doesn't 'feel' at all the same to play), the organ has its enthusiasts who continue to contribute marvellous music to the pop scene.

30 Write the part in chord symbols (*) or notes, or a mixture of both.

Organ writing is not like piano or synth writing – there's no sustain pedal, for one thing: try playing a regular keyboard without using the pedal and you'll see what a difference that alone makes!

So be careful when writing notes – if it can't be done smoothly without pedal, it can't be done.

If I were writing for organ, I'd stick to chord symbols wherever possible.

31 Use a double stave:

range

organs have all sorts of ranges, but by sticking to this you'll be OK. If the instrument has pedals you can write lower: consult your player

Basic technical info

32 Electric organs work on various systems according to their make:

Hammonds have so-called 'drawbars', which are basically individual sounds, each with its own fader (vol control) – so you can mix sounds together in any proportion.

Most other brands have buttons giving preset 'stops' (= one sound).

33 All organs have programmable settings.

So you can save a sound consisting of several 'stops' or drawbars and retrieve it at the touch of a button.

34 Most organs have two keyboards ('manuals').

These are set one above the other, so you can set an 'accompaniment sound' on one and a 'solo' sound on the other, playing one keyboard with each hand.

35 Organs have a volume pedal.

Called a swell pedal, it is built-in, foot-operated, and works exactly like a guitar or keyboard volume pedal.

36 Many organs have pedals.

They are set out like a keyboard and played with the feet. If your player is good with the pedals, then you have a bass player and keyboard player in one!

37 A 'Leslie' unit is used to give a distinctive vibrato effect.

All organs have a vibrato button, but if your player has a Leslie, a particular sound is available: it is literally **analogue phasing**, because the sound is put through a cabinet containing revolving speakers! The Leslie effect is adjustable – slow to fast (and medium).

38 4' (four-foot) = soft, 8' (eight-foot) = medium, 16' (sixteen-foot) = loud (these are called 'registrations')

All makes of organ have their own names for sounds; some names overlap between brands. Every make of organ sounds different – experts can instantly recognize which they are listening to.

This makes it difficult for the arranger to specify exactly what sound he wants (but *consult your player!*)

And there is a simple solution (see above): all the organs **group** their sounds by loudness (this piece of info is not strictly accurate* but it works). So, to let the organist know what you want –

39 Specify the registration you want as above, and add some instructions in words.

e.g. shouting, raunchy, lyrical, misty . . .

---

* Actually the figures 4', 8' and 16' refer to the *length* of the pipes on a traditional church organ – a system the electric organs borrowed. A four-foot pipe (4') would be an octave *higher* than an eight-foot pipe (8'): but on scores and parts the system is used for loudness.

Basic organ licks

Once again, it is impossible to give all the idiomatic ways of playing organ; but here are one or two nice things – this is not a complete list!

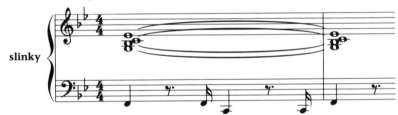

7 Guitar

The guitar and its cousin instruments have always been a part of popular music all over the world: the Spanish guitar in Europe and South America, the oud and banjo in Africa, the bouzouki in Greece and Turkey, the balalaika in Russia, the sitar in India, various versions of the same idea in China, Japan, Bali and the Far East, and no doubt others elsewhere.

With the invention of the electric guitar in the USA in the 1930s the instrument swept the world afresh.

1 **In popular music most guitarists can manage a variety of styles.**
A jazz player will have a good stab at rock, a reggae player will know some folk licks.

However, classical players are usually *useless* at all popular styles.

The can't read chord symbols and they can't improvise. *And* they can sound most un-funky.

2 **Write the part in chord symbols (*) or notes, or a mixture of both.**
Use notes for melodies only. Don't try to write chords out as notes. If you want particular voicings, use 'high shapes', 'med-high shapes' or 'low shapes'.

3 **The six strings of the guitar are tuned as follows:**

The bottom string is sometimes tuned down to D, especially by folk and classical players.

4 **Use a single stave with a treble clef. Write notes an octave above what you want to hear.**

The treble clef should have a small *8* attached to the bottom, to show that the music sounds an octave lower. This is not essential.

range
(concert
pitch)

written

5 **You can get higher notes than the above by using harmonics.**
By touching a string very lightly with the left hand while you pick, you can get a pure, whistling note. The easiest notes are the octave harmonics of the open strings, but many others, much higher than the normal range, are easily available. Consult your player!
Notate:

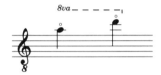

The sign *8va* .... means 'Play notes an octave above what's written'.

6 **There is a notation for guitar chord symbols called 'tablature'.**
You may come across it in song copies. It looks like this:

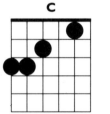
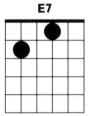

I personally have never met a player who prefers to use this notation. (It could be useful to give a player a specific **shape** for a given chord, but it's much simpler to write 'F ^maj7^ high shape', 'med-high shape' or 'low shape'. The players prefer that.)

Tablature is tricky to write if you're not a guitar player. The players can all use chord symbols. All in all, I don't recommend that you mess with tablature.

Electric guitar

The electric guitar was first used in jazz and rhythm-and-blues (the black American music which spawned rock 'n' roll). With the advent of rock in the 1950s it quickly took centre-stage.

It was for years the main instrument in all rock bands. Nowadays rivalled by the synth, it will never be totally eclipsed because synths (which are wonderful at what they do) can't do what guitars do – slides, picking, hard strums, hammering-down – all the techniques which make the sound of a guitar inimitable.

Besides which, *a guitar looks sexy.*

7 There are two basic types of electric guitar: solid-bodied and hollow-bodied (semi-acoustic).

The early jazz electric guitars were 'cello' acoustics (see **18** below) with pickups added. These are still made, and produce a beautiful mellow sound.

Solid bodies came later and have the advantage that you can turn them up louder before they 'feed back'. They have a rather more strident basic sound, very useful in rock and jazz-funk.

8 Different types and makes of guitar give enormous varieties of sound.

There are particular makes of guitar whose basic sounds are well known. Experts listening 'blind' can pick the sound of a Fender Stratocaster, a Gibson Les Paul, or any of a number of other types. Many lesser guitar manufacturers produce copies of the famous brands.

Your player may own more than one guitar. Listen to the sounds they make and choose the one that most fits your arrangement.

9 In addition to their natural sound, electric guitars can get a wide range of different sounds by using fx boxes.

Some of the most common are:

Distort	This used to be called fuzz, which describes the sound rather well: heavy and gutsy.
Phasing	This adds an attractive churning sound, rather like a non-pitch vibrato.
Flange	This gives notes an extra ping, and provides a filter-sweep effect.
Chorus	This doubles the sound, as if more than one guitar was playing in unison.
Envelope	This puts a blip on the front of each note, not unlike a quack.

All these fx can be adjusted to give more or less effect.

10 There are also effects that don't need boxes.

Feedback	Normally undesirable, this is used by guitarists for the screaming, climactic sound you often hear.
Stopped	By putting the heel of the right hand against the strings as you pick, you get a very short, stuffy sound (called *etouffé* by classical players).

Pitch-bend	Slides up from the pitch of the note, and back down again. You can't pitch-bend downwards.
Tremolo arm	Some guitars have a lever which causes the note to go both up and down, either slowly (like pitch-bend) or fast (tremolo).
Bottleneck	This is a metal tube which fits over a finger of the player's left hand. It is used instead of the fingers to get chord-shapes. Naturally, since it is a straight bar, it can get very few shapes, but it does give a very interesting, glidy effect.

I won't go into other guitar-playing techniques in detail. If you know about them, ask for them in words.

11 Traditionally there are two types of electric guitar style: lead guitar and rhythm guitar.

Lead guitar

12 The lead guitar plays mainly melodies and improvised solos.
They should *both* be marked SOLO on the part:

Notice, in the above example, the *thick lines* leading up to one note and down from another. These tell the player to do a **slide.** The technical term is the Italian *glissando.*

13 Write in words the style you want the solo to be in.
This applies even when the notes are written out, because the style will give the player the idea of what sound to use.

Use words like mellow, lyrical, hard, raunchy, funky, jazz, blues, country, etc.

14 Write in words the sound you want, if you know.
BUT listen to what the player suggests – she or he may have ideas you find you prefer.

Use words like strat, Les Paul, feedback, distort, phase, flange, chorus, etc.

The first two sounds above are makes of guitar. Don't use them unless you know the sound you're asking for.

The rest are the names of fx, see **9** and **10** above.

15 **At times when it is not soloing, the lead guitar can be used for melodic fills or high-shape comping.**

(Comping is short for 'accompanying' – playing the chords of the arrangement behind any melody or solo.)

While the rhythm guitar will always be the main comping guitar, the lead guitar can add richness to the texture by doing a melodic fill or a higher chord-shape as well.

If you want the lead guitar to comp, say so on the part.

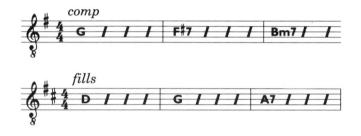

Rhythm guitar

16 **The rhythm guitar's main job is to comp.**

(Comping is short for 'Accompanying' – playing the chords of the arrangement behind any melody or solo.)

You don't have to tell the rhythm guitar to comp unless you have called her or his part 'Guitar 2', in which case she or he will need to be informed that this is a rhythm part.

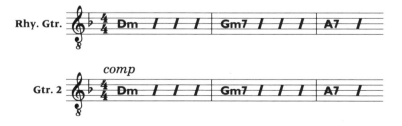

17 All the rhythm player needs to be told is the style of the music.
Even this may be obvious in some bands – they know their own style!

Here are some styles you could suggest in words: jazz, reggae, funk, hard rock, off-beat short strum, country, disco, ballad, blues, heavy metal, etc.

18 Rhythm guitar doesn't have to play all the time!
Put some rests in occasionally, and change the texture.

Acoustic guitar

The acoustic guitar was well established in popular music long before the invention of the electric guitar. To this day the playing style has retained much of the folk roots of its history – Spanish, Latin, hillbilly and American folk.

The blues and jazz are the other guitar roots, and they work equally well on acoustic or electric.

19 There are three broad groups of acoustic guitar: nylon-strung (Spanish), steel-strung and twelve-string.
Within these groupings there are many types of instrument. Let's take steel-strung as an example: we have the 'cello' guitar used in swing bands, so called because it has f-holes, not the usual round one; the folk guitar in all shapes and sizes; the 'Dobro', a guitar with a round steel disk for a front; and others.

But broadly speaking, within each group the instruments do roughly the same job.

29 Nylon-strung guitar: soft-toned
This lovely instrument, used mainly in Latin-American and Spanish music, has too soft a sound to compete with any but the smallest and quietest groups. Unless you mic it up (see **23** below).

For soft Latin music like the bossa nova it is a wonderful melody instrument, and its way of comping is very individual.

(Comping is short for 'accompanying' – playing the chords of the arrangement behind any melody or solo.)

Unlike other guitars the nylon-strung is often played with the fingers or fingernails instead of a pick.

21 Steel-strung guitar: a) folk. The two main styles are strumming and picking.
Strumming gives a rhythmic chordal backing to the music. There are many basic patterns. Consult your player.
Picking gives a lyrical, open feel. Again, there are innumerable patterns. Consult your player.

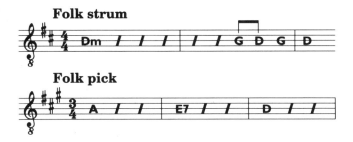

Some people write the word 'arpegg.' (= play arpeggios) instead of 'pick'. Just so you know.

A steel-strung acoustic can be played quite loud but it won't cut through a loud band. Unless it's mic'd up (see **23** below).

In folk music the steel-strung guitar is sometimes played with the fingers or fingernails instead of a pick.

22 Steel-strung guitar: b) blues. The two main modes are solo and backing.
Your player will either be able to do this or not. Many good players don't. Consult your player!

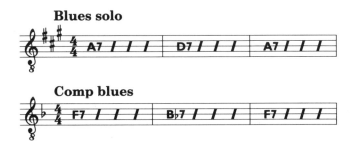

You *could* write melodies and mark them 'blues style'. I've never seen it done, and I wonder how a player would react. I'm not banning it, though.

Some blues-style players and Dobro players are adept with the bottleneck (see **10** above).

A steel-strung acoustic can be played quite loud but it won't cut through a loud band. Unless it's mic'd up (see **24** below).

23 Twelve-string guitar

This is a large steel-strung acoustic guitar with two strings tuned to the same note for every one on a normal guitar. The top (four) pairs of strings are actually in octaves, not unison. This gives an enormously big sound, a bit twangy but almost orchestral in richness.

Twelve-string guitars (having twelve strings) take a long time to tune up. Don't ask your player to grab one in mid-gig and expect it to be in tune. Actually even the most carefully tuned twelve-string rarely sounds exactly right. It's all 'part of the twelve-string sound'!

Twelve-string is used mostly for strumming, but it can sound good doing a pick or even a single line.

24 Mic-ing up an acoustic guitar

a) As I mentioned above, some acoustic guitars come with pickups as well. These can be plugged into an amp just like an electric.

b) You can buy contact mics for acoustic guitars. These are attached to the body of the instrument, often with special double-sided sticky-tape. They then plug into an amp.

c) In studio situations you can mic up an acoustic with an ordinary microphone. In live situations this method runs into a lot of problems because the dratted mic *will* insist on picking up the rest of the band as well. So you still can't hear the acoustic, and you run the added risk of feedback.

Other guitars and related instruments

25 Electric pedal steel guitar (Hawaiian guitar)

This instrument doesn't look much like a guitar at all and can only be played by a specialist. It isn't even held in the hands, but is mounted on a table-like stand. The player uses a metal bar instead of her/his left hand to produce different pitches, and the chord-shape is changed by foot-pedals which alter the tuning of the whole guitar.

Pedal steel guitar is widely used in Hawaiian music and country-and-western.

Write melodies or chord symbols for pedal steel. Remember that the slow slide is a main feature of the style.

The *thick lines* in the example show the player where to slide or pedal.

26 Banjo

The banjo is a steel-strung four- or five-stringed instrument whose body is round and covered in vellum or plastic.

Its distinctive, metallic sound is heard in blue-grass music, where its practitioners have developed a virtuosic picking style, and in traditional jazz, where it is more often strummed.

Write chord symbols for banjo.

27 Ukelele and banjolele

The ukelele or uke is a tiny four-stringed nylon-strung guitar from Hawaii. It is tuned much like the top four strings of a regular guitar.

The uke is mainly used in novelty music. In the 1930s an English comedian named George Formby made it famous.

The banjolele was a small banjo tuned like a uke.

Write chord symbols for the ukelele and banjolele.

28 Sitar

This very beautiful Indian instrument presents the arranger with enormous problems because the player will very rarely know Western music notation. So you can't write anything down for her or him except in words.

More than ever, *consult your player!*

29 Balalaika, bouzouki, oud, etc.

To be honest, I know very little about these instruments. I once wrote a melody for bouzouki, which I wrote out like guitar music (i.e., an octave above where I wanted to hear it). The player did it with no problem.

So: write melodies like guitar music.

I don't know whether players of these instruments know chord symbols.

Consult your player!

PERCUSSION

UNFREE

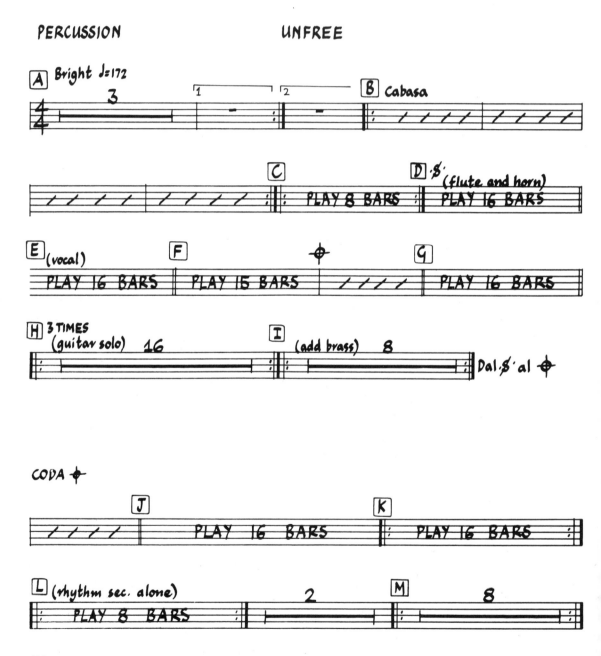

8 | Percussion

For arranging purposes we can divide up percussion into four types.

1) Untuned percussion used as part of the rhythm section: due to its Latin-American roots it is called Latin percussion or LA percussion
2) Untuned percussion used for occasional emphasis
3) Tuned percussion (vibes, tubular bells, timpani, etc.)
4) Synth percussion

Latin percussion

If you have a percussion player available, she or he can add various textures to the drum pattern in the rhythm section.

This is widely done in musics around the world; salsa from South America; high life from South Africa; reggae; disco and its offshoot jazz fusion; also in film and TV music.

1 Write the part with slashes. No clef is needed.

Don't try to write out a rhythm unless you *specifically* want it. The player will know a better one than you can dream up, nine times out of ten, and will in any case be funkier at her/his own rhythms than ones you impose.

2 To suggest a rhythm you can use cross or ordinary note-heads. Write the notes all on one pitch without a clef.

This example suggests a rhythm to be continued (the player won't do it slavishly on and on, thank goodness!).

3 Dream up a flavour (salsa means sauce!).

Use your imagination to make weird and wonderful rhythm sounds with drums and percussion.

Sometimes use only percussion.

Get your drummer to be a second percussion player: make complex textures with two percussion and no drums.

4 Consult your player!

Your player will own a selection of instruments. She or he knows best what they are. Add her or his imagination to yours in dreaming up nice sounds.

5 If you can't 'hear' it, don't write it!

In **2** and **3** above you have the two methods of adding percussion to your rhythm section: your imagination and your percussionist's experience and help.

Never write for an instrument you don't know in the hope that it will add some colour or other. That way lie disaster and embarrassment.

6 The most common Latin percussion instruments are listed here:

African drums	Deep-pitched, rather soft, tom-tom-like instruments
agogo bells	Two small cowbells joined together
bongos	Small single-skinned drums struck with the player's hands
cabasa	Beads stretched over a gourd, or metal beads over a metal canister
castanets	Spanish wooden clickers
chocollo	See shaker
claves	Two pieces of hardwood clicked together
congas	Large single-skinned drums struck with the player's hands
cowbells	Metal bells which don't ring at all – they go 'dok'
guiro	A hollow box with ridges cut into it, which are scraped with a stick
jaw's harp or jew's harp	A metal spring twanged in the player's mouth
kalimba	Metal strips held over a hollow box; the strips are twanged
maracas	Gourds filled with beads, which are shaken; a kind of shaker

sand blocks	Sand-paper stapled to blocks of wood and scraped together
shaker (various sizes)	Any container with beads or seeds inside; another name for chocollo
skulls	Same as temple blocks
sleigh bells	Little bells on a leather strap, which are shaken
tablas	Deliciously gluggy Indian drums
tambourine	A small drum with bells attached which is shaken or struck
temple blocks	Hollow wooden spheres struck with a beater; another name for skulls
triangle	A triangle of metal, tinkled with a beater
wood block(s)	Hollow pieces of wood, struck with a beater

There are lots of others, some of which your player may have. *Consult your player!*

Untuned percussion: general

7 **The other use for untuned percussion is as an occasional sound to emphasize or comment on the music.**

8 **The most common untuned percussion instruments (apart from Latin) are:**

bass drum (abbreviated to BD or Orch. BD)	A large deep drum, bigger than the one in a drum kit, hit with a padded beater
bell tree (see **12** below for notation)	Twenty or more bells of different sizes, mounted on a bar. Scraped with a beater, they give a long tinkling noise of rising or falling pitch. Individual bells can also be hit
cymbals	You can crash two cymbals together (crash cymbals), or hit one on a stand as in a drum kit (stand cymbal). You can use various beaters or a brush on a stand cymbal
finger cymbals	Pairs of tiny cymbals which tinkle when hit together
flexatone (see **12** below for notation)	A large spring with beaters attached, makes a wobbly bell sound. Good players can get a tune out of it!
klaxon	An old car horn honked with a rubber bulb
mark tree (see **12** below for notation)	A series of metal rods (large to small), hung by strings from a wooden bar. Makes a rich, complex ringing sound
roto toms	Like tom-toms but tunable (strictly speaking tuned percussion)
side drum	A large snare drum with a military sound

slap stick	Same as whip
tam-tam	An enormous gong with an explosive sound which rings for a long time. Can be damped for shorter notes. Smaller tam-tams also available
vibraslap	A sprung rattle which vibrates when hit. Originally an ass's jawbone!
whip	Two strips of wood hinged at one end. Makes a snapping sound like a whipcrack
wind chimes (see **12** below for notation)	Metal or wooden rods hung by strings from a board. Shaken, they tinkle prettily

Most of the Latin percussion instruments can also be used as general untuned percussion.

9 **Write the part with cross/diamond or ordinary note-heads. No clef is needed.**

10 **If you want your percussionist to play more than one instrument in a short space of time, write different instruments on different lines/spaces of the stave.**

11 **If you are asking a player to play more than one instrument, give her/him time to change!**
The above example could only be done at slow tempo, because the player has to put down two side drum-sticks and pick up a bass drum beater, then possibly move to the bass drum (depending on how her or his instruments are laid out).

12 **Instruments with lengthy, random sounds can be notated graphically.**

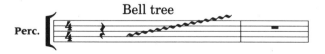

This means play the bell tree on an upward run. Start on beat two and fill the rest of the bar.

This kind of notation applies to bell tree, mark tree, flexatone and wind chimes.

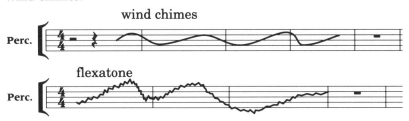

13 On the drums, cymbals and tam-tams you can sustain a note by doing a trill or 'tremolando'.

For percussion, trill and tremolando (tr and trem) mean exactly the same thing – sustain the sound by constant swift beating.

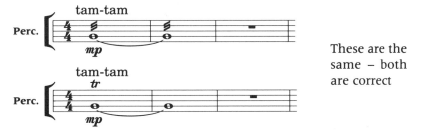

These are the same – both are correct

14 A tie (going to nothing) will tell the player to let the instrument ring.

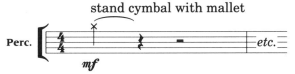

You can also write LV (let vibrate, or in French *laissez vibrer*).

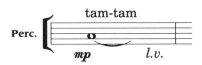

This is often used for instruments which ring for a long time.

15 The word 'damp' instructs the player to stop the instrument ringing.

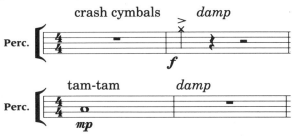

In the second example the player lets the tam-tam ring for one bar and then damps it.

16 General tips

Don't forget that percussion instruments can play softly as well as loud. They often sound gorgeous.

Be sparing with percussion. Larding it all over the place makes the music sound cluttered and makes your player tear about like Charlie Chaplin in a (not-so-silent) movie!

I'll say it again: if you can't 'hear' it, don't write it! Never write for an instrument you don't know and hope that it will add some colour or other. That way lie disaster and embarrassment.

Consult your player!

Tuned percussion

Some tuned instruments can be used as solo instruments. Others (e.g. vibes) sometimes even appear in the rhythm section. Other tuned instruments (e.g. timpani) are used for emphasis and colour.

17 Vibraphone (vibes)

range

Vibes have metal notes played with medium-soft mallets. Good players can use two in each hand, giving four-part chords.

Not all four-part chords are available, only narrowly-spaced ones. Consult your player!

The vibes has a vibrato effect done with a motor. It can be off or on, and the speed of the vibrato can be varied (not during playing).

The vibes has a sustain pedal which works just like a piano. There's no need to specify the use of the pedal in the first example above. The player would use the pedal for legato; in the second example she or he would hit the chord with no pedal.

You can write chord sequences (*) for a vibes player, who can comp (accompany) or solo.

18 Xylophone, marimba, xylorimba

These instruments have wooden notes and don't sustain.

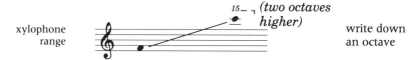

xylophone range   write down
                                                                                   an octave

The xylophone is played with hard beaters and has a clicky sound.

marimba range   write at
                                                                                   pitch in the
                                                                                   treble clef

The marimba is played with soft beaters and has a gluggy sound.

xylorimba range

The xylorimba is a xylophone and marimba combined into one very long instrument.

Write as for a xylophone or a marimba, specifying which.

You sustain on these instruments with trills/tremolandos.

19 Glockenspiel

This is a very high-pitched instrument with metal notes. Played with medium beaters.

Write for it in this range – it will
sound two octaves higher. It sustains
a little naturally.

20 Timpani (kettle drums)

These deep drums are played with felt-tipped beaters. They come in
four sizes.

They are tuned with a pedal. The note can be changed within a
second or so.

In an orchestra there would be three or four timpani, so you would
get the whole melodic range.

Percussionists in bands don't often have that many timpani (if they
have one it will be a 28"), and as they're enormous things to cart
around, may not be willing to bring them on a gig. Or only for extra
money!

In the above passage a player with three drums would have to change
with the pedals, twice.

The middle drum would be tuned to the first A, the top drum to
the D and the bottom one to the F♯.

The player would have to change the bottom drum from F♯ to G♯.
You might hear that happen – like a glissando – unless the player
damped it first.

She or he would then have to change the top drum to E.

The above passage is *very* difficult, even at slow tempo!

You can do rolls on the timpani, marked like a trill.

You can deliberately use the pedal to get glissando effects.

The last is struck once and then pedalled down before it dies out (about one second).

21 Tubular bells

These are long metal tubes, held in a rack and struck with a wooden mallet.

They cannot be written very fast.

is OK at medium tempo

22 Other instruments

Your player might own some less common instruments such as tuned gongs, gamelan, hand bells or glass harmonica.

Consult her or him as to ranges and notation.

Synth percussion

23 Percussion sounds, tuned and untuned, are very well done on many synths.

Most drum machines have some percussion sounds as well as drums.

If you have a sequencer or drum machine, you can write for synth percussion just like synth drums.

See 'Synth drums' in Chapter 4, and 'Sequencing' in Chapter 9.

9 Electronics: Signal Processing

The effects

Signal processing means adding an effect to a sound electronically.

The use of signal processing in the recording studio is not within the scope of this book. However, many effects can be added live, if the band has them available. Here are the most commonly used ones.

For guitar fx boxes, please see Chapter 7.

1 Reverb
Reverb is the addition of general atmospheric echo to the music. (Delay is a repeat of each note.)

Reverb is good on lead vocals, and on almost everything if you are in a very 'dry' (un-echo-y) room.

Reverb is adjustable. *Be sparing!*

2 Delay
Delay means an audible repeat of each note (reverb is general echo).

You can have a single delay or lots of repeats. The repeats can fade out or continue indefinitely. It's all adjustable. Experiment!

3 Chorus, chorusing
Chorusing thickens the sound to make it appear that two instruments are playing in unison. (So a voice sounds like a chorus.)

Except with synths, electric guitars and bass guitars, chorusing is not as brilliant in live situations as in recording, as the audience will get 'acoustic' sound from the instrument or voice you're trying to chorus, spoiling the effect. But it can be useful as a thickener.

4 Phasing, flanging
Phasing and flanging are two different but similar effects which put various kinds of wobble on the sound.

They are good for enriching brass, guitars and keyboards. You could use them on other sounds too, though this is less usual.

Phasing and flanging are adjustable. Experiment! Except with synths, electric guitars and bass guitars, the effect will be less noticeable live than in the recording studio, due to acoustic 'spill'.

5 Gated reverb

This is an effect which gives the start of a reverb which is sharply cut off. You hear it on heavy metal and other records, especially on the snare drum sound and on lead vocals.

It also works on any short, stabby sound like brass.

6 Slap echo

Slap echo is actually a very fast single delay.

Useful on vocals, brass and other sounds with a strong attack.

Don't use on drums!! It throws out the beat something awful!

7 Harmonizing

Harmonizing allows a voice or instrument to play two (or even three) notes at once, electronically. You set it at a fixed interval (say an octave below, or a third above) and then anything you sing or play comes out both at the pitch you play and at the preset interval above or below.

So if you set it at a fifth above (+ seven semitones)

Certain harmonizers will do two transpositions at once:

+ 7 semitones
– 3 semitones

Some harmonizers can be programmed through MIDI to change the interval of transposition while you play. It's not as yet a very subtle technique, and you usually hear 'blips'.

Sampling

8 Sampling is recording any sound (a door slam, a telephone ring, a french horn note) and playing it back from a synth keyboard.

Once you've programmed the synth (sampler) you can play the noise or note at any pitch, simply by playing up and down the keyboard.

9 **So, for instance, you would make a new complete drum kit by sampling the sounds in your house.** Door slam for bass drum, wine glass for cymbals, bed-springs for tom-toms, etc.

10 **Or you could make a new melody instrument from the squeak of a rusty hinge.**

11 **Samplers are also very useful for synth-like processes, faking strings, brass, harp, flute and all sorts of instruments. Consult your player!**

12 **Sampling is a subject which needs a whole book to itself, but if you know someone who has a sampler, you can write for it.**

13 **For sampled unpitched noises, write exactly as if it were a percussion instrument (see Chapter 8).**

14 **For melodies, write a synth part.**
For all possibilities, **consult your player!**

Sequencing: the theory

15 **Sequencing is computerized arranging for synths. An electronic memory remembers the notes and rhythms you play, and plays them back at the touch of a button.**
On all but the simplest sequencers you can correct mistakes afterwards, and tidy up the rhythm if you've played sloppily.

16 **The simplest sequencer is a drum machine.**
A drum machine is an electronic box containing drum sounds (often sampled) and a memory. You can play in an entire song's drum part and it will be stored ready to play back at any time. On most machines, songs can be saved to floppy disk, so your band's entire drum parts could be stored and used at will.

17 **Some synths come with a built-in sequencer.**
These sequencers will play any sounds the synth can make, melodies and chords, not just drum sounds. Songs are saved to floppy disk and can be reloaded and played at any time.

18 **Most built-in sequencers can be patched (= connected) by MIDI cables to other MIDI instruments.**
So you can link up two or three synths, a drum machine and a MIDI wind controller, and they'll all play automatically in time with each other.
You can of course program them to play separate parts – they don't all have to play the same thing.

19 The most versatile and complex sequencers come as computer software.
You MIDI-connect your computer to all your MIDI instruments, and the computer acts as a control 'brain', playing back whatever you've played in.

20 Some computer sequences will print out the music!

Writing for sequencer

(See also Chapter 3, **10–15**).

21 If you personally are programming the sequencer as part of the arrangement, there's no need to write out a part.
Just program the sequencer and save to disk. There it is. Who needs music?

If you're writing out a full score (*) of the arrangement, you'll need to show what the sequencer is playing.

There's some useful shorthand here. You show the *kind of thing* the sequenced synth is playing for a bar or two, then write 'sim' or 'simile' (Italian for 'the same kind of thing') and revert to a chord sequence (*).

Saves a lot of time.

This doesn't work for melodies, of course.

22 If you are expecting someone else to program the sequencer, you'll have to write out a full part.

Write exactly as you would for the real instrument.
(See Chapter 4 for an explanation of the above notation.)

UNFREE

90

10 Brass and Reeds

I have grouped brass and reeds together because very often they play together. As well as all the saxophones, flute and clarinet are included here because in rock, jazz and pop it is the sax players who also play ('double') them.

Transposing instruments

1 Some instruments transpose.
Annoying as it may seem, some instruments (including most brass and reeds) are built so that their 'scale of C' – i.e., the easiest scale to play on that instrument – is not C on the keyboard. So when you write a middle C for them, they play not middle C but some other note.

For instance, the trumpet plays a B♭ when a C is written. The trumpet is said to be a transposing instrument 'in B♭'.

2 Write at concert pitch in the score or lead sheet, but transpose the part.
In order for the player of a transposing instrument to play what you want to hear, you have to write it out for her or him in a different key. Crazy, I know.

(But if you're making a score or lead sheet of your arrangement, do yourself a favour and write all the instruments in concert pitch – normal keyboard pitch – then at least you can read what you wrote!)

3 If an instrument transposes 'down' a tone, you must transpose the part 'up' a tone.
The trumpet transposes down into B♭, so if you write a tune in C, she or he plays it in B♭. TO MAKE A TRUMPET PLAY A TUNE IN C YOU HAVE TO WRITE IT OUT IN D!

The system is: however many semitones an instrument transposes in one direction, you must transpose the part the same number of semitones in the other.

Brass ranges and transpositions

4 Trumpet – transposes (*) down into B♭

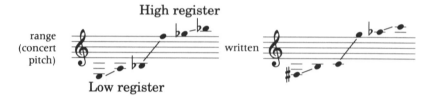

A 'lead trumpet' player is a high note specialist: she or he can go up higher than marked (consult your player).

> **IMPORTANT:** *No* **trumpet player likes playing high all the time without a rest. It wears them out, so that after only twenty minutes or so** *they can't play any more.* **Don't write continuously in the high register, and do provide plenty of rests.**

This rule can be relaxed on a recording overdub, when players can record in short 'takes' with rests in between.

5 Flugelhorn – transposes (*) down into B♭

The flugelhorn is roughly the same size as the trumpet, slightly larger and with a duller, warmer tone. It doesn't go quite as high as the trumpet. Flugelhorns are played as a 'double' by the trumpet players.

In the high register it's difficult to play perfectly in tune: remember this when scoring for flugelhorn within a brass section.

6 French horn – transposes (*) down into F

The french horn is often called just 'the horn', but that is also the pet-name that most brass and reed players give their instruments – 'my horn' – so to avoid confusion here I will always say 'french horn'.

The french horn reads music in both bass and treble clefs. You will find it convenient to write for it in both, even when you're writing in concert pitch.

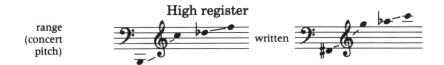

High register

range
(concert
pitch)

written

7 Trombone (full name: tenor trombone) – plays at concert pitch

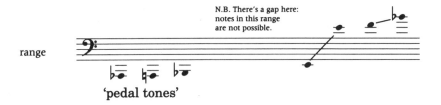

range

N.B. There's a gap here: notes in this range are not possible.

'pedal tones'

High-note specialists can go (sometimes much) higher than this: consult your player.

No matter how high the music goes, always use the bass clef. Symphony players are used to the 'tenor clef' for high music, but rock, jazz and pop players don't like it.

IMPORTANT: *No trombone player likes playing high all the time without a rest. It wears players out so that after only twenty minutes or so* they can't play any more. **Don't write continuously in the high register, and do provide plenty of rests.**

This rule can be relaxed on a recording overdub, when players can record in short 'takes' with rests in between.

8 Bass trombone – plays at concert pitch

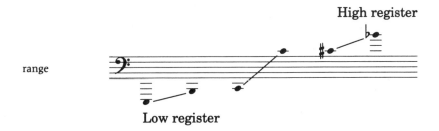

High register

range

Low register

9 Tuba – plays at concert pitch

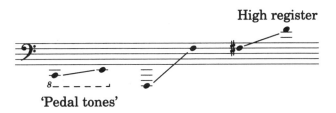

High register

'Pedal tones'

Writing for brass

10 If you're writing chord symbols for improvisation, transpose the chords just as you would the notes.

11 When writing a part, put in lots of rests.
Brass players really do tire. Have them (at most) play thirty-two bars, then rest for sixteen. When you look at your finished arrangement, if any brass instrument is playing for more than two-thirds of the total length, you've over-written it.

12 Trumpet, agile; flugelhorn, sprightly; french horn, quite agile but slow-speaking; trombone, not very agile; tuba, surprisingly agile
You can write extremely fast passages for trumpets:

A similar passage (written lower, of course) would work well for french horns, but would sound smooth where the trumpets were crisp.

I *might* score this kind of music for flugelhorns, but only in the knowledge that I was writing uncharacteristically.

Trombones can't do this kind of thing at all because of their slides. You'd end up with a smear of sound – which may be what you want, it's very trombonistic – but if you do, write it like this:

The lines tell the player to slide down from the printed note (you can also slide up). The technical term for this is *glissando* or *gliss*.

Valve trombone: this is a trombone fitted with valves. It is more adept at agile passage-work than the slide trombone, though at the cost of a rather thinner tone.

Tubas can play amazing things like this:

13 Trumpet, warm; flugelhorn, fat; french horn, velvety; trombone, rich; tuba, tubby

This counts as good trumpet, flugelhorn or french horn writing (the trumpets can do it higher as well, the french horns lower as well):

Trombones doing this is one of the richest sounds in all music:

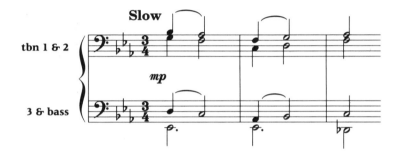

14 Mutes

for trumpet	straight; tin; bucket; plunger; harmon
for french horn	straight; hand-stopping (see **21** below)
for trombone	straight; bucket; plunger
for tuba	straight

There are no mutes for flugelhorn.

Straight mute gives a thin, toppy, nasal sound.

Tin mute is similar but not so edgy.

Bucket mute gives a fuller sound, rather like the open (unmuted) instrument 'with a cold'.

Plunger (wah-wah) mute is not inserted in the bell but held in the hand. It is passed across the bell during playing to give the wah-wah effect.

Harmon mute is the tightest mute, giving a very small, constricted sound. There are two different noises, the second (slightly warmer) being produced by removing the 'tube' from the centre of the mute.

Notation for mutes:
Don't forget to give enough rest before and after a muted section for
the player to pick it up and put it down.

15 Fluttertongue, growling

a) **Fluttertongue** is an effect available on all brass instruments (you
can also get it on a flute) where the player does a 'rolled R' into the
mouthpiece while blowing. The sound is like a musical 'raspberry'.

b) **Growling** it mostly done on trumpets, often aided by the plunger
mute. It sounds like the brass equivalent of Satchmo's singing.

The trumpet section

(All examples written at concert pitch.)

16 Solo/trumpet/unison trumpets

Imagine the difference in sound between these lines played solo, or
by two (or three) trumpets:

bebop

17 Two trumpets

pop

Latin

18 Three trumpets/four trumpets

Three or four is the usual number in a larger section.

pop

rock

salsa

disco

bebop

The french horn section
(All examples at concert pitch except where marked.)

19 Solo french horn/unison french horn

Imagine the difference in sound between these lines played solo or by two or three french horns:

Unison horns doing an upward 'whoop' is an exciting sound:

20 Low register

Low notes on french horns are rather weak but extremely beautiful. Carefully scored, they make a soft alternative to low trombones:

21 Hand-stopping the french horn

The player stuffs her or his hand down the bell. This gives an effect exactly like muting *and raises the pitch of the instrument by a semitone.* You can do it while playing – even during a note. NB, when this is done the note will slide up a semitone.

Notation:

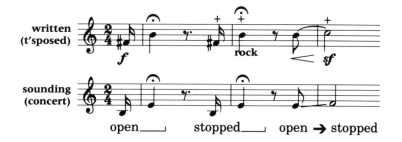

The trombone section

22 Solo trombone/unison trombones

Imagine the difference in sound between these lines played solo, or by two (or three) trombones:

23 Two trombones + bass trombone/three trombones + bass trombone

24 Low register

Trombones are very good at doing 'pedal notes' and low chords:

25 Tuba can be added to the trombone section.

The sound is fatter than bass trombone, and weightier.

Tubas can't play long phrases without having to stop for breath. Don't write anything that lasts more than about five seconds without a breath.

Tubas are much more agile than (especially bass) trombones.

Reeds ranges and transpositions

26 Flute – plays at concert pitch

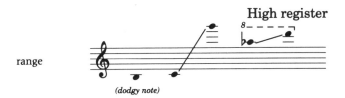

The **piccolo** plays an octave higher than the flute. It transposes up an octave, so write the music an octave below what you want to hear, both on the part and in the score. The piccolo's bottom note is D, not B.

The **alto flute** transposes (*) down into G:

You would only use it for its rich and breathy bottom register – the first one and a half octaves, say – because above that it is no different from the regular flute.

The **bass flute** transposes (*) down the octave:

27 Clarinet – transposes (*) down to B♭

There are also clarinets in A, C, D and E♭: you are most unlikely to meet them in rock, jazz or pop music.

The **bass clarinet** in B♭ (often 'doubled' by clarinettists) plays exactly an octave below the clarinet, and makes a warm, reedy sound. It transposes (*) down more than an octave, and the player always reads in the treble clef.

28 Soprano sax – transposes (*) down to B♭.

This is the advisable range within which to write – players will go higher with great ease when improvising, but will give you a funny look if you write up there.

29 Alto sax – transposes (*) down to E♭

This is the advisable range within which to write – players will go higher with great ease when improvising, but will give you a funny look if you write up there.

30 Tenor sax – transposes (*) down more than an octave to B♭

This is the advisable range within which to write – players will go higher with great ease when improvising, but will give you a funny look if you write up there.

31 Baritone sax – transposes (*) down more than an octave to E♭

This is the advisable range within which to write – players will go higher with great ease when improvising, but will give you a funny look if you write up there.

Writing for reeds

32 When writing chord symbols (*) for improvisation, transpose the chords just as you would the notes.

33 The saxes, solo (all examples written at concert pitch)
Soprano has a strident sound which can be very passionate, or soft and intimate in the lower register.

Alto is creamy, very soulful and gutsy.

Tenor can honk in a '50s rock band, croon a ballad or blast out a jazz solo.

Baritone has a tough, nutty sound suitable for solo work as well as section parts.

Having said this, every player has an *individual* sound. The sax is the instrument most capable of tonal variation (apart from synths). Know your player, write well for your player.

34 Unison saxes (all examples written at concert pitch)

When you write unison lines, you can mix saxes with no problem; so if you have only two to play with, say an alto and a tenor, they'll blend well. Make sure that what you write falls within each one's range:

35 The sax section (all examples written at concert pitch)

Some typical kinds of sax writing (not a full list!):

36 Flutes and clarinets (all examples written at concert pitch)

Flutes can be used as a lighter kind of trumpet section sound:

Solo flute is a very airy sound (this line would also sound good, though different, on unison flutes):

Alto flute gives a sultry feel (this line would also sound good, though different, on unison alto flutes):

Bass flute has an almost ethnic flavour (this line would also sound good, though different, on unison bass flutes):

Clarinet is used in the older jazz forms:

Bass clarinet can be a snake or a siren:

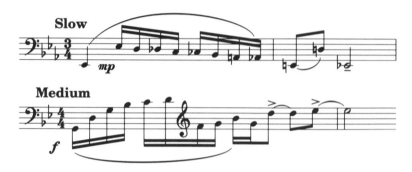

Combining brass and reeds

(All examples written at concert pitch.)

37 If you have just two or three 'blowers' at your disposal, there are various ways of combining them:

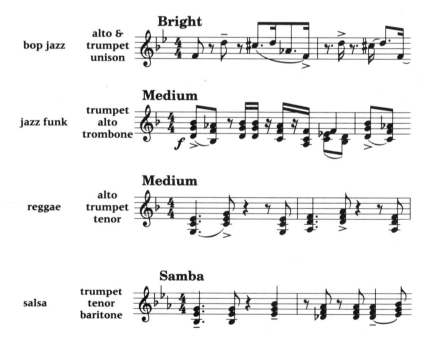

38 If you have several each of brass and reeds, you can combine together or separately.

Brass and reeds together, layered:

Brass and reeds together, mixed:

Brass and reeds separately:

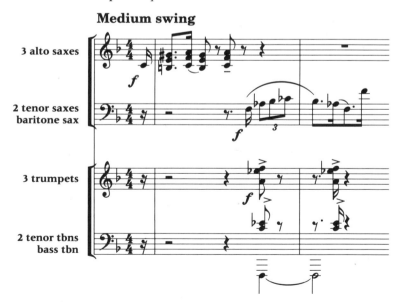

39 By introducing the less usual instruments you can get a totally different sound world.

This is the kind of scoring first invented by the great jazz arranger Gil Evans:

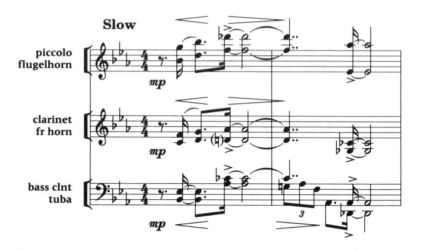

Evans also made use of symphony instruments such as oboe (*), cor anglais (*), bassoon (*), piccolo trumpet (*) and harp (*).

Synth brass and reeds

40 Choose whether or not you want it to sound reasonably like the real thing.

You can use synth brass and reeds exactly as you like – as long as you like what you hear, it doesn't make a damn of difference.

Some synth 'brass' and 'reeds' sound more lifelike than others. If you have a choice, choose the one you like the sound of, even if it isn't the most lifelike.

Try playing some sounds: you'll find that playing synth brass or reeds outside the range of real brass or reeds can sound great – *but not like brass or reeds.* You'll find that playing licks which a brass or reed player couldn't do can sound great – *but not like real brass or reeds.*

The choice is yours. Neither method is 'wrong'. (Nothing is 'wrong' if it works – except boring or your listeners or tiring your players.)

41 'Realistic' brass

(I won't show you the other kind – you can find it yourself.)

The range rule is, don't normally go above about C:

You can use just the right hand if it sounds better.
You *can* go higher for a 'lead trumpet' sound:

42 'Realistic' reeds

If you have a sampler(*) you can get really good 'saxes'. Write just as
you would for real saxes, but remember that the more idiomatic slurs
and smears won't be there. Safe top note is about F (top line, treble
stave):

43 'Realistic' flutes

Flutes is a sound that synths are particularly good at. All sorts: African
flute, wooden flute, calliope, pan-pipes, Japanese flute – these are
some of the names you'll find, and the sounds are equally exotic.

filmscore

44 Other 'instruments'

Some presets you get on synths sound extremely unlifelike, but they can be useful nevertheless. I have a synth with a particularly awful 'oboe' on it – but the bass end is a wonderful bassoon sound. (The actual 'bassoon' on the same synth is naff.)

Don't let your imagination be stifled by the name a manufacturer gives a sound. It may be a naff 'trumpet' but it might sound great for some other use. Listen to the sound, not the name.

VIOLINS A

UNFREE

Strings

a) Writing for strings is dead easy. Just write something down and they'll play it.

b) Writing for strings is a skilled craft. Great composers have spent a lifetime perfecting it.

Both these statements are true.

Ranges

1 There are four instruments in the string orchestra.
The **violin** (or fiddle) is the highest in pitch. A string orchestra usually has two lots of violins – first and second violins. A string quartet also has two violins (plus a viola and cello). Abbreviation: vln.

The **viola** is lower in pitch but is still small enough to be held under the player's chin. It has a nutty, wiry-but-warm sound. Abbreviation: vla.

The **cello** (pronounced 'chello', full name violoncello – double-check that spelling!) has a deep velvet sound and is played held between the legs. Abbreviation: vcl. Plural: cellos or celli.

The **double bass** (or string bass, or contrabass) is so big that it is played standing up, or sitting on a high stool. Abbreviations: cb, db.

2 Violin

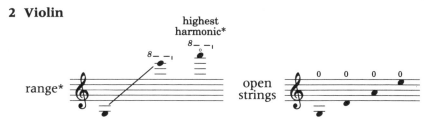

* See **9** below for an explanation of harmonics and their notation

3 Viola

The viola gives all arrangers a headache because its music is written in an old clef, the **alto clef.**

alto clef   this note is middle C

When the viola's music goes high you can use the good old treble clef.

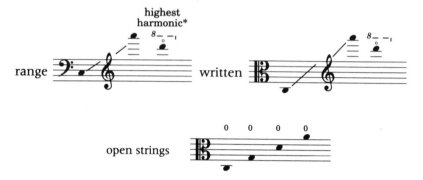

range   written

open strings

4 Cello

The main clef is the bass. When the music goes high you *could* use another old clef, the **tenor clef:**

tenor clef   this note is middle C

– but cellists all read the treble clef, so don't bust a gut.

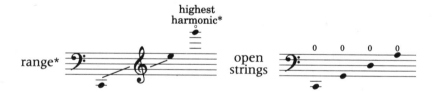

range*   open strings

5 Double bass

(For double bass as used in a rhythm section see 'String bass' in Chapter 5. Why I call it double bass in a string section and string bass in a rhythm section I don't know!)

The double bass plays an octave lower than the notes you write. So write everything an octave higher than what you want to hear. If you are writing a score, it is correct to write an octave higher there too.

---

* See **9** below for an explanation of harmonics and their notation.

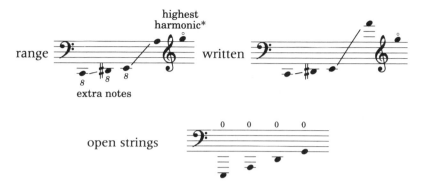

For high music bassists read the treble clef. But they don't like going high.

String-playing techniques

All the stringed instruments can do all these techniques.

6 Bowed ('arco')

This is the standard mode of playing for stringed instruments. If you mark nothing on the part, this is how they'll play (not true for rhythm section string bass – see   Chapter 5).

To make them return to bowing after a passage doing something else, write *arco*.

7 Bowing/phrasing

In string music phrase-marks have a special significance: they indicate to the player that all the notes under one phrase-mark are to be played within one stroke of the bow:

You don't have to tell the player whether to do an **up-bow** (weak attack) or a **down-bow** (strong attack) – she or he will do as a matter of course what the music demands: but if you want to do so, the notation is:

ᴠ   up-bow

⊓   down-bow

8 Tremolando

This is a tremolo effect done by moving the bow a tiny distance back and forward, very fast.

* See **9** below for an explanation of harmonics and their notation.

Notation:

9 Harmonics

By touching the string very lightly while you bow you get a pure, high whistling note. The easiest notes to get are the octave harmonics of the open strings, and many others are available.

Using a technique called **stopped harmonics** you can get the whole chromatic scale, starting two octaves above the bottom open string, and going up incredibly high.

Don't specify which kind of harmonics you want – the player will do the most convenient.

Notation:

The letter 'o' is also used to indicate an open string (this has a raw sound and of course no vibrato – an effect you might want to specify):

10 Double-stopping (two-note chords)

Strings can play two notes at once. Because of the arrangement of their open strings, only certain combinations of notes are possible:

a) any two notes including one of the top three open strings and another note up to a fifth *below* it (double bass, a fourth).

b) any two notes including one of the bottom three open strings and another note a fifth or more *above* it (double bass, a fourth).

c) any two notes making an interval between a minor third (*) and an octave (for the double bass, double-stops not using an open string are difficult and not very useful).

If this is confusing (as I expect it is), consult your player.

11 Three- and four-note chords

Strings can play chords containing notes up to the number of their strings, *but because their finger-boards and bridges are curved, not flat, chords of more than two notes will be 'spread'*.

It is impossible to tell you here what all the possible three- and four-note chords are. There are very many of these, though the choice *is* limited by the design of the instruments and the players' hands. Here are just some of those you can get on the violin (for the viola and cello the basic shapes are the same; on the double bass the technique is difficult and not very useful):

These basic shapes can be played in most keys.

For four-note chords keep the bottom note within the bottom eight semitones of whichever instrument you're writing for.

For three-note chords you can write much (at least an octave) higher. Consult your player.

12 Broken chords

Any group of notes which can be played as a chord can be played as a broken chord:

13 Plucking (pizzicato)

Plucking is done with the fingers, and string players are not generally very fast at it – not nearly as fast as guitar players.

That said, you can write most things pizzicato that you can write bowed: runs, double-stops, chords. No tremolandos (well, the composer Elgar did do it), no harmonics (well, a few – consult your player), *definitely* no sustained notes (well actually, plucked notes *can* be sustained for a very short while – for a second, say).

Notation:

Arco tells the player to start using the bow again.

Bartók pizzicato: this is when the player pulls the string away from the fingerboard and snaps it back; so you get a whiplash sound as well as a very short, loud note.

Notation:

14 The mute (sordino)

String mutes fit over the bridge, and make the sound softer and rather muffled. A whole string section muted is a dreamy sound.

Notation: (*con sord*: 'with mute'; *senza sord*: 'without mute')

Don't forget to give the player rests in which to put on and take off the mute.

15 'Sul ponticello' ('pont' for short)

The player bows the strings very close to the bridge, producing a thin glassy sound.

Write *norm.* (back to normal) when you want the *ponticello* to end.

The string section

The string section can sustain everything from a simple high melody or a drone bassline through to the entire texture of a piece.

16 High melody

The violins can carry the melody of your arrangement, either in unison:

or in octaves:

17 High counter-melody

The same technique can be used to put a simple tune, high in the violins, against the main tune somewhere else in the arrangement.

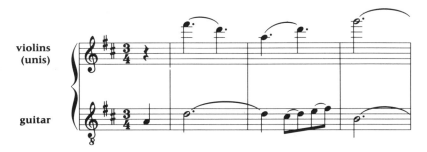

18 Melody (not high)

If the melody is lower than the above examples you can use the violas, or the violas and celli, for the lower octave:

A particularly rich sound is achieved by putting all the strings (except the double basses) in absolute unison. The range can't go below the violin's bottom note, or above the cello's comfortable playing range, so:

19 'Footballs'

This is the term used to denote a texture of chords made up of long notes (semibreves or 'footballs'). These are very useful to give a lush 'cushion' of sound in the background of your arrangement.

20 Shimmer

Not dissimilar to 'footballs', this effect uses the violins and sometimes also high violas playing long chords, **tremolando** (see **8** above).

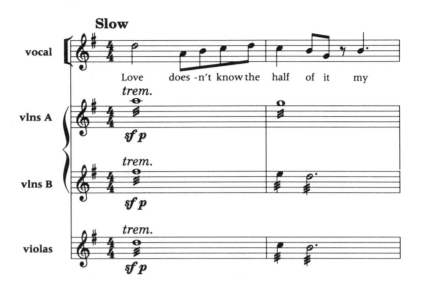

21 High broken chords

For more energetic music you can use the high strings in arpeggiated passage-work (ha! long words for something simple).

22 Stab chords

23 Heavy rhythms

String players, being classically trained, don't do rock rhythms particularly well (their swing jazz feel is even worse). However, this kind of thing is not beyond them:

24 Bassline thickening

This gives a ponderous, even portentous feeling.

* This will sound in octaves; see **27** below.

A held 'drone' or 'pedal tone' is most effective where the harmony permits it:

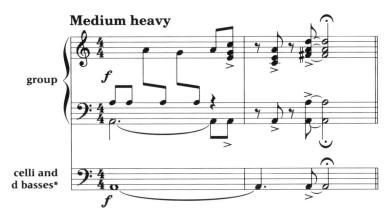

25 The upward/downward rush

String players learn their scales and can play them very fast. Don't bother working out how many hemi-demi-semis there are in your run, just start it off, giving the players an idea of which scale they have to play, and leave it to them!

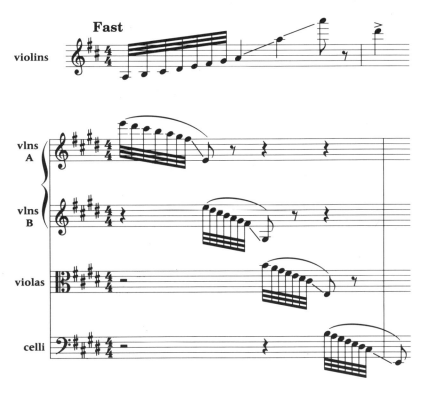

---

* This will sound in octaves; see **27** below.

26 Pizzicato (plucking)

Violins in unison:

Low strings, as a melody or as a bassline:

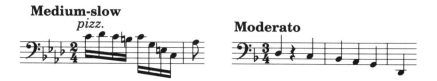

The whole section:

27 Complete backing

I shan't give any examples of this. Suffice it to say that almost any backing that you can play on a keyboard will sound good on a string orchestra, except highly rhythmic stuff.

There are loads of string textures you can pirate from classical music. A look at the miniature score of Vivaldi's Four Seasons will suggest a couple of dozen different ones, for a start. Copy any sound you've heard anywhere, or imagine new sounds of your own. See also Chapter 13.

28 Write the celli and double basses as one line, and it will come out in octaves.

Obviously this only works if you want the celli and basses to play the same line – but you'll find you often do. It saves arm-ache for the arranger!

For examples of this see **24** above.

Solo String Techniques

29 All the stringed instruments can play solo in the classical style.
A solo violin at the tear-jerking moment of a movie is such a cliché
that I need hardly mention it. But there are lots of other uses for solo
violin – use your imagination.

A lot of TV programmes use a solo cello for a yearning, nostalgic feel.

Solo viola and solo double bass are far less common – but if you think
you can write for one, go ahead. The player will love you for it! (Not
if you go too high on either instrument; a viola in the high violin
register just sounds like a straining violin: not nice. A double bass
above concert middle C is a disaster area.)

Remember, both the viola and the double bass are reasonably
quiet instruments and are soon drowned out by any but the thinnest
scoring.

30 Solo strings may need to be mic'd-up.
Where a string orchestra will make itself heard over a loudish group,
solo strings won't, unless they're mic'd-up. Some string players own
'contact mics' which they can plug straight into a guitar amp.

31 Folk and ethnic violin
There are several folk styles for the violin (or fiddle as it's often
known in this context):

> Irish fiddle (jigs, etc.)
> Gypsy (Hungarian goulash music!)
> Country-and-western fiddle (hoe-down)
> Indo-Pakistani violin (improvised)
> Jazz violin

Write in any of these styles *only* if you know a player. Consult your
player (she or he may not read music!)

32 String quartet, etc.
Yes, folks, it's good old 'Yesterday' time! Seriously, the sound of a
group of solo strings is unlike anything else and can be very useful.

You can write for any group of solo strings you have available.
Here are some of the traditional groupings – but don't worry, I only
list them for reference. Any grouping will work.

String trio (violin, viola, cello)
String quartet (two violins, viola, cello)
String quintet (two violins, two violas, cello; or two violins, viola,
   two celli; or two violins, viola, cello, bass)
String sextet (two violins, two violas, two celli)
String octet (double string quartet)

I shan't give any examples of writing for solo groups. Suffice it to say that almost any backing that you can play on a keyboard will sound good on solo strings, except highly rhythmic stuff.

There are loads of string textures you can pirate from classical music. A look at the miniature score of any of Beethoven's, Mozart's or (wow!) Bartók's quartets will suggest lots of different ones. Copy any sound you've heard anywhere, or imagine new sounds of your own.

Talking of Bartók, don't forget the even more 'modernistic' sounds you can do with strings – sounds made by composers such as Ligeti and Penderecki, which were used for movies such as *Jaws, Psycho* and *The Exorcist*.

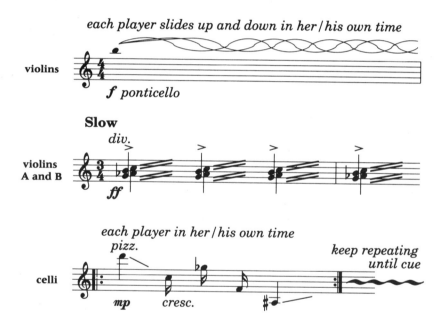

The lines in these examples tell the players to slide around in the direction of the lines. The technical term is *glissando* (*gliss* for short).

Don't just slavishly copy these few examples. In fact, don't just slavishly copy *any* of the examples in this book!

Synth strings

33 Synth strings can sound 'lifelike' or obviously synthesized. Both kinds are good.

The designers of synth string sounds often come up with nice sounds that don't really sound a lot like real strings. Lots of groups use these sounds for their own good qualities.

34 Use synth strings as 'strings' or as synth sounds.

Nobody says you *have* to use any synth sound for what it's intended for. Use your imagination, and have the sound do something else.

·Or use the sound in the same way as you would strings. If it still sounds like a synth but does the job OK, fine.

35 *Or* try to get as lifelike a 'string' sound as possible from your synth.

The rest of this section will concern itself with doing this.

36 Synths can be good at simulating string sounds; but they can't simulate the articulation.

Stringed instruments have a design which affects the way they sound. They have four strings, tuned a fifth (or a fourth) apart, and they are fingered by four of the fingers of the player's left hand, moving up, down and across the fingerboard.

They are played with a bow, or plucked.

They have no frets. Players can therefore adjust their tuning slightly to give a sweeter or a brighter tuning. This they do, all the time.

This produces the distinctive way we hear stringed instruments *move from note to note*. There is no way a keyboard instrument can simulate these things.

37 So 'orchestral strings' synth sounds better than 'solo strings' synth.

The articulations of real orchestral strings are disguised somewhat by their large numbers. This gives the designers of string synth sounds a better chance.

38 Synth strings are good at the following:

The best synth strings will do the list below. Experiment with your particular synth to see what it is best at.

High counter-melody (**17** above) I haven't put 'high melody' because if you draw attention to the string sound by giving it the tune, on most synths it would be noticeable.

'Footballs'	(**19** above)	The 'wash' of string sound is the most usual string synth application.
Shimmer	(**20** above)	Some synths now have a splendid 'tremolando' sound.
Bassline thickening	(**24** above)	
Pizzicato	(**26** above)	

39 Don't get side-tracked into a search for a perfect 'string' sound.
The search for the absolutely lifelike string sound on a synth is prob-ably a fruitless one. Be open to the possibility that the sound you have found might do the job you want perfectly well, despite the fact that it doesn't sound too 'realistic'.

40 A nice 'string sound' that is obviously synthesized can sound better than a sound which aims to be realistic and just misses.
Don't have the embarrassment of your listener saying 'The string sound isn't very good, is it?'

12 Orchestral and other Instruments

The following instruments do not appear in any standard popular music band. However, you may know a player and decide to use her or his skills.

In film and TV writing these instruments are much used.

For strings, see Chapter 11.

For orchestral percussion, see Chapter 8.

Unless marked, all instruments play at concert pitch.

In alphabetical order:

1 Accordion

There are two playing methods for the accordion. The right hand has a keyboard like a piano for melodies and simple chords. The left hand has a set of buttons which play preset chords(*). You can do major, minor, seventh and diminished in all keys.

Write on one stave with notes and/or chord symbols (*)

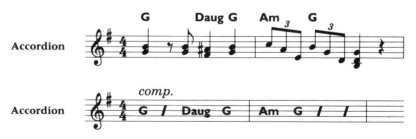

('Comp' means 'play accompaniment'.)

2 Alto flute – see Chapter 10.

3 Bass clarinet – see Chapter 10.

4 Bass flute – see Chapter 10.

5 Bassoon
The bassoon is the bass instrument of the double-reed family. It has no mouthpiece, but two reeds tied together.

The bassoon is reasonably agile except in its top range, where playing is more difficult but the sound is a beautiful 'falsetto'.

The bassoon won't cut through a band unless you amplify it. Best for soft textures. Blends well with french horns.

The **contra bassoon** is a really deep instrument, an octave below the bassoon. It has no useful upper register.

Transposes (*) down an octave

6 Bass trombone – see Chapter 10

7 Blues harp – see 'Harmonica', **14** below

8 Clarinet – see Chapter 10

9 Cor anglais – also called **English horn**
Despite being called a horn, this is actually a deep-pitched oboe. The sound is softer than that produced by any instrument except the flute, very rich and ponderous.

Transposes (*) down into F

A reasonably agile instrument, use it for its bottom one and a half octaves. Above that an oboe is usually better.

10 Cornet

The cornet is just like a trumpet, except that its tubing is conical, not cylindrical. It has a sweeter tone than the trumpet, and is used a lot in brass bands.

Transposes (*) down into B♭

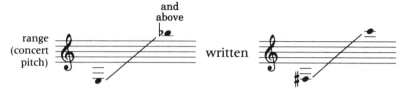

Write exactly as for trumpet, bearing in mind the rather softer sound.

11 Flugelhorn – see Chapter 10

12 Flute – see Chapter 10

13 French horn – see Chapter 10

14 Harmonica – also called **mouth organ** or **blues harp**

There are two instruments here: a) the diatonic **mouth organ** (blues harp) and b) the **chromatic harmonica**.

a) The **mouth organ** (blues harp) is a small suck-blow instrument from which good players can get the most amazing bends and growls. It plays only a major scale: simple chords made of thirds or single notes.

Mouth organs are made in all keys. For blues playing you use one which is a fifth below the key you're playing in – this gives the blues seventh rather than the major seventh.

Write melodies and/or chord symbols (*).

Actually this could confuse the player because she or he is playing an instrument in a different key (a fifth down – here in C). But transposing is risky too. The truth is that mouth organ players generally play by ear.

Consult your player!

b) The **chromatic harmonica** is a larger instrument with a button on the end which gives all the semitones of the scale. Its 'open' scale is usually C, sometimes G or F. The scale it gives with the button pushed is a semitone higher. It plays simple chords made of thirds or single notes.

Write using notes and/or chord symbols (*).

15 Harp

range

Write on a double stave, like piano music. Some players can read chord symbols (*).

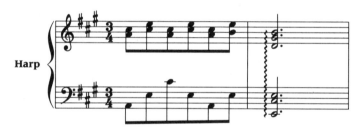

Harp

The wavy line before the chord in the second bar tells the player to 'spread' the chord (i.e., play each note consecutively very fast from bottom to top).

The old cliché for harp writing (none the worse for that!) is the glissando (fast run) – shortened to 'gliss'.

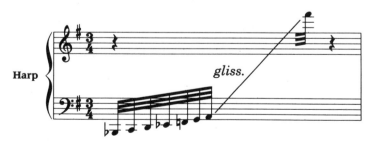

Harp

Start writing the scale out in demi-semiquavers, until you've given all the required notes once. Then write a thick line to the top note you want.

By putting a crotchet rest at the end of the bar, I've told the player to make the gliss last for three beats.

Up-and-down glisses are written as follows.

The harp can do quite complex things, almost like a piano, but with the following provisos:

It can only play (up to) eight notes at once, four to each hand. The spacing of the chords (four notes to each chord) has to be written within one octave per hand because the player can't stretch further.

It takes time to change key on a harp. You only have seven pitches available at any one time (all octaves). So you might have this ready:

– now, to play a G natural takes a pedal change.

To play a chord for C major 7   takes three pedal changes!

General rule of thumb: write simpler for the harp than for a keyboard instrument. Consult your player!

16 Mouth organ – see 'Harmonica', **14** above

17 Oboe

The oboe is a double-reed instrument. It has no mouthpiece, but two reeds tied together. This gives it a nasal quality.

The oboe is quite an agile instrument. Its bottom notes are harsh and difficult to play. If you want a harsh sound, fine. If not, write low stuff for cor anglais (*).

The oboe won't be heard in a band unless you amplify it.

18 Piccolo – see Chapter 10

19 Piccolo trumpet – also called D trumpet

A small trumpet used by classical players for high notes. A rock or jazz lead trumpet player will go just as high or higher on a conventional trumpet, but it won't sound as pure.

Transposes up, usually to D

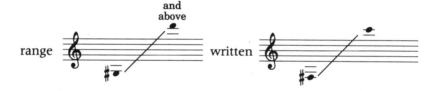

20 Pipes

Including pan-pipes, tin whistles, etc.

These instruments come in specific keys and can only do the major scale of that key. Write for all these instruments transposed into C major. If you stay within this **written** range:

– the player will do it at whatever pitch is best for the pipe.

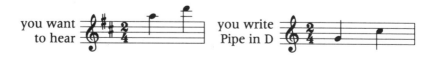

21 Recorders

Here are all the recorders (and more) you'll ever meet. (The descant is the common one used in schools.) Write for them in the following ranges:

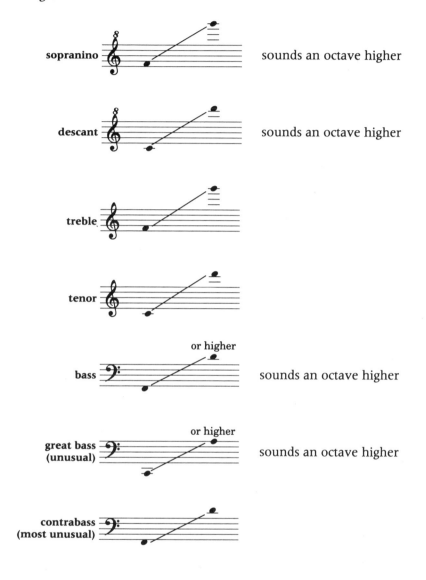

sopranino — sounds an octave higher

descant — sounds an octave higher

treble

tenor

bass — sounds an octave higher

great bass (unusual) — sounds an octave higher

contrabass (most unusual)

22 Trombone – see Chapter 10.

23 Tuba – see Chapter 10.

13 A capella

A capella means any music played with no rhythm section. An a capella group is a group with no rhythm section:

A choir

A small number of solo singers

A quartet of saxophones

A string orchestra

A jazz band, minus its rhythm section

Any instrumental and/or vocal group

I'm dividing this chapter into two sections: a capella music which is highly rhythmic and behaves as if it had a rhythm section; and a capella music which is in the ballad style – not in strict tempo.

Strict tempo a capella

1 **You have to replace the missing rhythm section from the players/singers you've got.**

You need a

bassline

rhythm/harmony

the tune

singers can also clap or snap their fingers

You can see that the above list corresponds to the classic rock or jazz lineup.

jazz	*rock*	*a capella*
double bass	bass guitar	bassline
piano	rhythm guitar	rhythm/harmony
sax/trumpet	lead guitar	the tune
drums	drums	clap/snap

2 Imagine what a rhythm section would play, and write it out for your a capella group.

The ∕. sign means play (or sing) the last bar again. Great shorthand! You can keep writing it for as long as you want the same bar repeated.

You can't, of course, transcribe* the drums in a capella. You just have to make sure there's enough going on rhythmically to fill the gap they leave.

Held chords and long silences can be death to a rhythmic a capella arrangement. The whole thing can sag.

BUT – short gaps and stops, in strict tempo, can be very exciting.

3 Work out a pattern on the keyboard or guitar, and then transcribe it for your group.
Here are some well-known piano pieces transcribed for a capella groups.

* Literally, 'write across'; it means write out for another instrument.

Für Elise (Beethoven)

(The french horn doubles the bass note to make his rhythm easier to play.)

Moonlight Sonata (Beethoven)

(Octave changes are necessary in the bass because of the ranges of the stringed instruments.)

Waltz (Chopin)

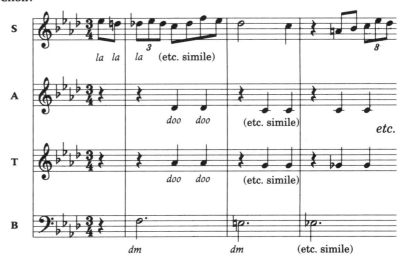

If you're writing scat (*) syllables which don't change, start each line off, then put ('etc. simile').

4 The deepest instrument or voice you have does the bassline.
It doesn't have to be a bass instrument: in a women's gospel group it would be the deepest female voice.

The $\frac{2}{\cdot}$ sign means sing (or play) the last two bars again. You can keep writing it for as long as you want the same two bars repeated.

5 A middle group of players or singers does the rhythm/harmony.
This important group both elaborates the time and gives the harmonies
of the music.

The rhythm gets built up into something quite complex. I've done a
mixture of 1) putting the rhythm/harmony in places where the bass
singer is silent, and 2) doubling the bass's rhythm. This makes up for
the absence of drums.

Some of the bass notes get doubled by the rhythm/harmony in the
above example. This is impossible to avoid with a group whose range
is so narrow. It's not a problem.

6 Add the tune to this:

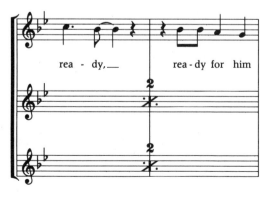

I added the instruction 'all clap on the offbeat' (the offbeat is beats two and four of the bar). That's all you need to put.

Most a capella singing groups work from memory in performance, and they'll fix the clapping themselves.

7 Here's the same thing arranged for saxophone quartet.
They can't clap!

(As this is a score I've not transposed (*) the parts – they're in concert pitch.)

Notice that I've put the bassline down an octave (because it's possible!)

Notice also that in the tenor sax part I've switched between the two lower voice parts of the original, so as to avoid doubling the same note.

8 At any point you could miss out any element of the texture.
Play the tune with only the bass
– or with only the rhythm/harmony
– or play the rhythm/harmony alone.

9 Some melodies are so rhythmic that you can arrange them in rhythmic unison.

Non-strict tempo a capella

The principal uses for this are:

Out-of-tempo section in ballads and other pieces (you can of course make the whole piece out-of-tempo)

TV and film music

Classical-style arranging

Out-of-tempo sections and pieces

10 Think in exactly the same way as for strict tempo, except that you can be much more lax with the rhythm.
Pauses and long held chords are fine in out-of-tempo sections. The tension doesn't have to be maintained (that's why it's out-of-tempo).
You do, however, have to keep the music *flowing*.

11 The simplest and easiest out-of-tempo section is solo piano or keyboard.

I've written the melody to be played, with the chord sequence (*) underneath.

I've instructed 'out-of-tempo', and 'solo' to tell the pianist she or he doesn't have to be in time with anybody else.

Where I want a specific voicing in the right hand, I've marked it.

When the melody is elsewhere and the keyboard has to comp (*), write in *colla voce* (pronounced 'collar vochay', Italian for 'with the voice'). This means 'the voice is out-of-tempo: follow the voice'. You don't have to write 'out-of-tempo' as well as *colla voce* on the piano part.

You write *colla voce* whether it's a voice or an instrument soloing.

(Classical writers put *colla parte* when it's an instrument. I've never seen that in a popular music score.)

Put in slashes in the chord sequence if there is no written melody in the part.

12 For larger numbers of instruments out-of-tempo, you'll need one player to lead, or a conductor.

This is quite usual. The leader of the group usually does it. But check in your mind whether your group has anyone competent to lead an out-of-tempo section, before you write one!

13 Work out a pattern on the keyboard or guitar, and then transcribe it for your group.

Exactly as in **3** above. Actually, since all those examples are classical pieces, they're very appropriate for out-of-tempo arrangements.

14 Fix a bassline, a harmonic filler and the tune; possibly a countermelody. Orchestrate!

You will know how you want it to sound.

The group you have will restrict your choices, but will provide (no matter how small it is) a great opportunity to use imaginative textures and voicings.

Don't be afraid to miss out instruments. You don't have to use the whole group.

For instance, strings accompany the voice more delicately than brass.

15 If the rhythm section is present, feel free to use it (out-of-tempo)!

If this is an out-of-tempo section in a group or band piece, let the players play if you want to.

- We've already looked at keyboard and piano.
- The drummer can shimmer on his cymbals or do quiet rolls on the tom-toms.
- The bass player can softly play an out-of-tempo bassline. If it's a string bass, she or he can use a bow.

TV and film music

We're straying beyond the edges of what this book is about here. However, I'll give some (perhaps rather vague) tips for those who find themselves working for TV or film.

16 Given the instruments you've got, you can write in any style.
TV and film music uses a lot of pastiche (music deliberately copying a well-known style, like honky-tonk piano or romantic classical).

If you are allowed to choose the instruments which will play your music, choose a group which will be able to play in the widest possible range of styles.

17 Under-write, don't over-write: there's a picture to watch!
Most first-time TV and film writers make their music too *interesting*! Remember, it has a supporting role here. It is the 'wallpaper' against which the actors act. Most film music you've heard, *you haven't noticed*! This is a good thing, not a bad one!

18 Be careful of dialogue, be subtle underneath it.
There are two rules of thumb here:
    a) Don't put anything noisily rhythmic or jumpy behind dialogue – it distracts the viewer from the dialogue.
    b) If possible, put the melody well away from the range of the human speaking voice. Then the dialogue and the music will be heard as separate, not competing.

19 Cynically use all the old movie music clichés – everyone else does!

    The 'she's in danger' grumbling bassline

    The 'driving along' pop song

    The 'car chase' rock brass and percussion

    The 'open meadow' flute theme

    The 'army manoeuvres' snare drum and orchestra

    The 'silent comedy' honky-tonk piano

    The 'romantic' classical piano concerto

    The 'Chariots of Fire' piano-and-synth track

etc., etc.

20 BUT do the main theme in your own personal style, and give it your best shot.
TV and film writing isn't (as I may have implied above) a second-rate craft. It's a skill, certainly. But if you put your very own style into it, your film or TV music will sound personal to you, and people will want to employ you.

Classical-style arranging: orchestration

This really is the subject of another whole book.

My problem is, anything I write here will be far too sketchy to cover this enormous subject.

General advice:

- Use the 'out-of-tempo' part of this chapter as a start.
- Listen to classical records, and get the miniature score from a music shop or library to see how the effects are done.
- Use the info elsewhere in this book for the ranges and techniques of the instruments. Most of the common orchestral instruments are to be found in various chapters: strings, brass, woodwind (in Chapter 10 and 12), percussion.

If you can imagine a sound, try to write it. You will learn more from trying it and getting it creatively wrong than from this or any textbook.

BLAZ DUES

Daryl Runswick

14 The Jazz Arrangement

Jazz music presents special opportunities to the arranger, which require special ways of writing.

I've divided the chapter into three sections:

The head arrangement

The small band arrangement

The big band arrangement

The head arrangement

On small band gigs, a head arrangement is often all that's needed.

1 **A head arrangement is simply the melody and chord sequence (*) of a tune.**
The routine (*) is not given, because on jazz gigs this is often arranged verbally:

e.g. 'Let the piano do an eight-bar intro; then into the tune, play it twice; then some choruses of trumpet, followed by sax, piano and bass; then the tune twice and end.'

2 **Since there's no routine, a lead sheet is not necessary.**
Just write out a set of parts.

3 **Write out the melody, and put the chord sequence (*) separately underneath.**
Soloists like a separate chord sequence to work from, so don't on this occasion copy the chords on to the music: put them underneath.
Blaz Dues is an example of this type of head arrangement.

Exception: if the lead instrument in the group is a keyboard or guitar, copy the chords with the melody.
Because the player will want to do tune and chords both at once.

4 Because trumpets, saxes, etc. are transposing instruments (*), you'll have to write out a set of parts.

The tune and chords in concert pitch are useful for piano, bass, guitar, trombone, flute, etc.

Another copy transposed for B♭ instruments will do for trumpet, tenor or soprano sax, clarinet, etc.

If you have an alto or baritone sax, a part transposed for E♭ instruments will have to be made.

5 You'll need a separate bass part.

a) For jazz-funk arrangements there will be a melodic bassline. Write it out in notes. If it's an unchanging bass lick, the player won't need chord symbols.

b) For straight jazz arrangements a chord sequence (*) may be all the bass player needs.

c) And there will be arrangements where both written music and a chord sequence are necessary.

6 The drum part should probably be written separately.

The drummer *could* play from a photocopy of the piano (or any) part – it contains all the information she or he needs: the length of the chorus and any phrasing which may need to be accented.

But not all drummers read music other than drum parts all that well. A drum part is preferable.

a) If there is no special accenting to be done, just give lengths in bars and the feel.

Swing

$\frac{4}{4}$ ‖:   8 bars   :‖   8 bars | 8 bars   ‖

The above is an 'aaba' (*) tune simply notated for the drums.

b) If there is accenting to be done, those bars will have to be marked out like a conventional drum part.

The small band arrangement

7 Arrangements for small bands (up to six players) can often be done as glorified head arrangements.

8 Jot down a routine (*) just for your own reference.

Here's an example of a routine you might do for a band consisting of trumpet, tenor sax, piano, bass and drums.

Blaz Dues
> Intro (piano) four bars
> Theme (trumpet and sax have separate parts)
> Repeat theme
> Sax solo
> Backing for sax solo
> Trumpet solo
> Backing for trumpet solo (same as above)
> Piano solo
> Theme
> Ending

The extra instructions you are giving the band, over and above a head arrangement, are:
> The intro
> The separate parts for the horns *
> The order of the solos
> The backings behind the solos
> The ending

In other words, quite a lot. Nevertheless, a glorified head arrangement layout will do all this.

9 Work out any separate melodic parts, backings for solos, etc.
In the arrangements routined above a bebop tune is played, mostly in thirds, by the trumpet and sax.

Work this out on rough paper, in concert pitch:

Bright

Work out the backing which will be played occasionally behind the solos:

* All blowing instruments in jazz can be called 'horns'.

10 Now copy out a set of parts, giving all the relevant information to each player.

Here's what the tenor sax part will look like, complete:

(Should you wish to play this piece with your band, the head arrangement, the full tenor part and the other partial hints above should enable you to reconstruct the whole piece. It's playable by any combo from a duo upwards. Be my guest.)

TENOR SAX   BLAZ DUES

SOLOS: SAX, TRUMPET, PIANO

BACKING (on cue) for trumpet solo:

On last theme, take Coda ⊕

The big band arrangement

If you're writing for more than about six instruments, write out a score or you'll lose track of what you're doing.

11 Jot down a routine (*) for your own reference.

Here's an example of a routine you might do for a band consisting of two trumpets, two trombones, alto sax, two tenors, one baritone, synth, bass guitar and drums.

Fazz Junk

a	eight bars	bass and drums only
a	eight bars	add synth, fills
a	eight bars	add trumpets and trombones, stabs
a	eight bars	add saxes, more stabs
a	two bars	drum break
a	eight bars	tune, trumpet and tenor sax
a	eight bars	repeat tune
b	eight bars	middle, synth and rhythm
a	eight bars	tune, trumpet and tenor sax
aaba		choruses, open, trombone solo, baritone sax solo, alto sax solo. Occasional backing (trumpets and tenors)
aaba	thirty-two bars	ensemble chorus
aaba	thirty-two bars	tune, as above
a	eight bars	with stabs, saxes and brass
a	eight bars	brass only
a	eight bars	rhythm only
a	eight bars	bass and drums only
ending	two bars	drum break and final stab

12 How can we shorten the job of writing this out?

Well, the first four sets of eight bars can be written out as one set of eight bars repeated four times.

You'll write out the score (*) with everybody playing, then mark the parts as follows:

Synth: play second x onwards

Brass: play third x onwards

Saxes: play fourth x onwards

(x means time or times, as in maths. Stupid, but it works.)

13 The 'aaba' of the tune has an obvious repeat built-in.
Do the two 'a' sections as one eight-bar repeat.

14 The solo choruses will have to be written out in full.
This is because you want to put repeats round the whole thirty-two bars.

   You will mark this passage 'round and round until cue'. This means, 'Keep repeating the thirty-two bars until all the solos finished, at which point the bandleader will cue you to move on.'

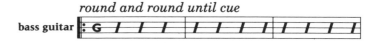

15 Plan to put the chords into the parts of all the soloists here.

16 For the occasional backing, plan to write it into this thirty-two-bar section, and mark it 'Play on cue only'.

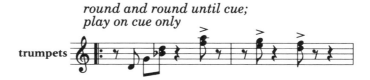

The two conflicting references to 'cue' will be a small problem, but the bandleader will explain to the players.

17 Now plan thirty-two bars for the ensemble chorus.

18 And now a Dal 𝄋 al ⊕ (*).
The tune is played as before, so we can send the players back to the 𝄋′ and then on to the coda.

19 The coda ⊕ is eight bars repeated four times.

Saxes play first x only
Brass play first x, 2nd x only   } as 12 above, in reverse!
Synth play first 3 x only

20 The ending will be written out.
So: an arrangement containing a minimum of 292 bars (depending on the length of the solos) has been reduced to a routined score of 108 bars.

21 Now to write out the score
– which is fully discussed in the next chapter.

15 The Full Score

Don't start a score until you've done a routine (*) or lead sheet (*)!

The vertical layout

1 **Work out how many lines you'll need on your score-paper.**
Count the number of instruments you're arranging for, taking the following things into account:

a) Some instruments need a double stave (keyboards, harp).

b) Some groups of instruments can share a stave, if their music is fairly simple (violins a and b, cellos and basses, trumpets 1–3, trombones 1–3, saxes, bvox, etc.). (You must write each player's own part out, of course.)

These calculations will give you the number of staves you need on your score-paper. Score-paper is available in single sheets (which I recommend) from music shops. You can get sizes including ten, twelve, sixteen, twenty-four, twenty eight and thirty staves.

Or you can carefully rule out one page of staves yourself, and photocopy it.

If you rule out your own score-paper, photocopy it once as it is to be used as a title-page. Then write on to your original the shortened instrument names, clefs, key signatures, brackets and bar-lines, and photocopy that for your main score pages.

Saves a lot of boredom and time!

See page 2 of my score *Unfree* for the kind of layout I mean.

2 **On the first page put the title plus the names of the composer, lyricist and arranger.**
Just as for a lead sheet (*). You'll notice that on my title-page I've moved the music down to the bottom of the page to make room for these details.

155

3 Plan to lay out your score with the rhythm section at the bottom; any vocals or lead instruments above that; and the rest of the band, grouped in families, how you like at the top.
This is only a recommendation. As long as you're tidy it doesn't matter that much. But if you're giving your score to a professional to read, they won't complain about the layout I've suggested.

4 On the title-page, write out in full detail the instruments and voices you are using.
I've left a gap on the left for this.

For instance I've written, not just '3 trombones' but '2 tenor trombones(*)', '1 bass trombone(*)'.

Similarly with the saxes, bvox*, lead vocal*, and guitar (electric)*.

I don't specify the percussion instruments here – I do it during the piece, wherever a new instrument is needed.

5 Use brackets to link related instruments.
At the left-hand side of each page I've used these on violins a and b (I could have done the whole string section: that would have been equally OK); on the flute and horn; which always play together; on the brass; and on the vocals.

I've also, of course, put a 'bow' bracket on the double-stave synth part.

6 Put clefs, key signatures and time signatures on all the staves.
YOU WILL BE WRITING THE SCORE AT CONCERT PITCH (*).

So the key signatures will all be the same.

The time signature goes on the first page only. The rest you must repeat throughout the score.

Don't write clefs or key signatures for the drums.

For percussion, only write clefs and key signatures if it's tuned (*).

7 Put in a tempo marking.
A word (slow, medium, bright, ballad, funk, etc.) may be enough. If you want to be specific, add a metronome speed (*) as well, or instead.

8 Rule out your bar-lines, linking groups of instruments for easier reading.
Don't make the bars too small for the music you're going to put in them!

9 For the rhythm section staves, one long bar-line would be confusing.

Which two lines are the double-stave of the synth part?

Bar the rhythm parts separately.

In my score I've used paper with more staves than I actually need, and I've left a blank stave between each group of instruments. This means that when a part goes very high (like the flute at letter $\boxed{\text{D}}$) it still looks good.

10 From page 2 onwards, label each stave, but not in full.

It is important to name the instruments and voices on every page, so that you or whoever's reading the score doesn't get confused.

But you don't need full details – abbreviations will do.

The bar-by-bar layout

11 Plan your layout using a routine (*) or lead sheet (*).

A score can be many pages long.

You WILL get confused unless you at least jot down a routine. A routine will also give you the best clues how to make your arrangement as short as possible, using repeats (*), first- and second-time boxes (*), Dal 𝄋 al coda (*), etc., etc.

12 I advise you to rule out the full score-page for every page, even when some instruments are not playing.

When you look at a published miniature score of a classical piece, the printer often saves space by reducing the score, for a page or two, to just those instruments which are playing at the time.

You can do this (it will certainly save paper), but I advise against it for two reasons:

a) When you, or the bandleader or conductor, are looking in a hurry for a certain instrument, it will always be on the same part of the page.

b) More important, if you decide later that you want to add, say, strings at letter $\boxed{\text{D}}$, the empty bars are there for you to use. (OK, you'll have to erase some rests.)

13 Put rehearsal letters, 𝄋 and ⊕ both above and below the score.

They're twice as noticeable then.

14 I advise that you put your first rehearsal letter │ A │ at the very start of the piece.

This is not always done; but if you wish later on in the arrangement to use reference bars (see **20–25.** below) back to bars 1–8, and if bars 1–8 don't have a letter, you can't do a reference.

15 Put rehearsal letters AT LEAST every sixteen bars.

In a rehearsal you don't want to be saying, 'Let's go from, wait a minute, er, fifteen, sixteen, seventeen bars after │ C │': it'll take you ages to count up, then the band have to count, and one of them'll get it wrong . . . That's a timewaster, and annoying for everybody.

16 Put first- and second-time boxes (*), Dal 𝄋 and DC al ⊕ above or near every group of instruments.

The more times you write these things, the more noticeable they are.

Somebody is going to be copying parts out from this score – things like this can get missed!

17 When doing repeats, you only need one different instrument to make first- and second-time boxes necessary.

In *Unfree* at bar four of letter │ A │ the drums do something different on the repeat. Nobody else is different. Nevertheless the whole score has to have the boxes.

A first-time box can be as many bars long as you like.

As soon as there is a difference in any part on the repeat, start a first-time box.

18 You must copy first- and second-time boxes into all the parts, even when there isn't any difference between them!

Because the bandleader will say, 'Let's go from the second-time bar in letter │ F │.'

If you haven't put the boxes in all the parts, half the band won't know what she or he is talking about.

UNFREE

Composed and arranged by Daryl Runswick

19 Play 1st x only; play 2nd x only; play on 𝄋 only; do not play on 𝄋; etc.

(x means time or times, as in maths. Stupid, but useful.)

These are good ways of saving time and paper. *Unfree* has a gradual build-up, adding instruments every eight or sixteen bars. At letter $\boxed{C}$ I've avoided having to write out an extra eight bars by putting 'play 2nd x only' on the trombone part.

You'll find other examples of this kind of thing throughout the score.

161

20 At the ⅀ write one bar out in full, with no ⁄ signs or slashes.

At letter ☐D☐ of *Unfree* I've written out the drum pattern again. The drums are already playing this pattern, so at first it doesn't seem necessary.

But this is the ⅀! At the end of the letter ☐I☐ the drummer is playing something different! So she or he needs to be reminded (on jumping back to ☐D☐) to change back to the old pattern.

Reference bars

21 To save score-writing time you can indicate that a bar copied out earlier in any part is to be played again.

BUT YOU CANNOT DO THIS IN THE INSTRUMENTAL PARTS!! YOU MAY ONLY DO IT IN THE SCORE.

When you copy out the parts you *must* write out in full any bars whih are cross-referenced in the score.

22 Find the earlier bar which is the same and write its rehearsal letter and bar-number inside a circle.

So the second bar of letter ☐C☐ is C2. (C2) is what you write in the new bar.

Starting at the second bar of ☐D☐ in *Unfree*, I've done this for the rhythm section.

23 If more than one instrument is repeating an earlier bar, draw a wavy line down from the reference through all the instruments concerned.

This only works with parts next to each other in the score.

At the second bar of ☐D☐ onwards I've done this for the synth, bass guitar, drums and percussion.

163

you,   un - free.   Set me

free, _____ set me

171

24 **You can refer different instruments back from the same bar to different places.**

Look at *Unfree*, letter F bar 9. The lower strings and brass are repeating bars from letter F while the rhythm section is repeating bars from letter C .

25 You can refer back to a whole section with one reference bar.

If (as in *Unfree*, letter $\boxed{\text{G}}$), the whole rhythm section plays sixteen

bars exactly as at letter $\boxed{\text{C}}$, you can write, all in one bar:

LETTER C

1–16

This only works if the whole arrangement does a sixteen-bar repeat
at the same time.

It doesn't have to be the *same* sixteen bars!

At letter $\boxed{\text{G}}$ the flute and horn are referred back to letter $\boxed{\text{D}}$

the guitar is referred back to letter $\boxed{\text{E}}$

the rhythm section is referred back to letter $\boxed{\text{C}}$

everyone else has sixteen bars' rest.

So it works.

26 Don't refer back to reference bars!

When you are copying out the parts you'll be confused and angry if
you come to a bar which says (**C2**), and on turning back to (**C2**) you
find (**A6**). Not cool.

27 Chords col (*col* is Italian for 'with').

You can save copying out a chord sequence (*) several times with this method.

See *Unfree*, letter ⌷ I ⌷. The guitar, synth and bass guitar all play the same chord sequence.

28 Write out the chords once (generally in the part with the stave highest in the score), then put 'chords col [that instrument]' and a wavy line along the other staves, for as long as the chords are the same.

chords col guitar

178

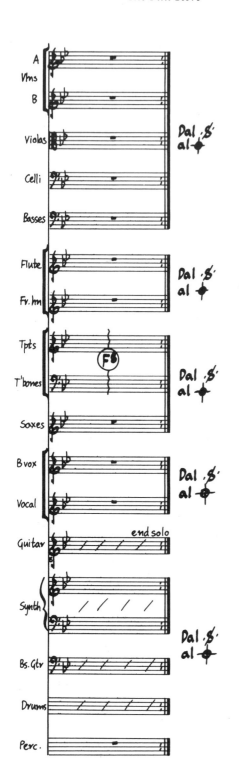

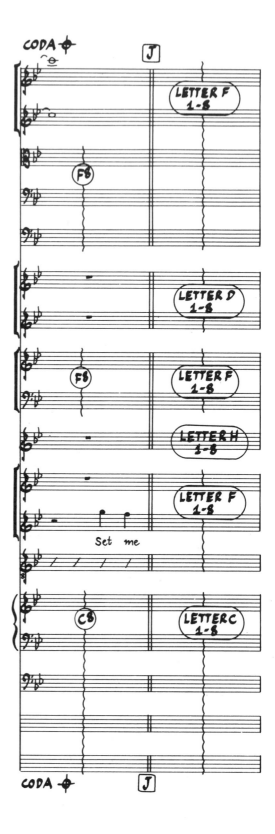

29 Make a noticeable space between the Dal 𝄋 and the coda ⊕.

I've put white space here. I did it by cutting, pasting and photocopying.

That's an eye-catching thing to do, but it isn't necessary. Just leave some space with empty staves in it and start again for the coda with a new 'left-hand edge'.

Or go to the next page.

30 Write 'end solo' to tell the player to stop soloing.

Obvious, but don't forget – even when (as at 2 before $\boxed{\textbf{M}}$), the solo is only two bars long!

I also put '(continue solo)' at letter $\boxed{\textbf{I}}$, to make it unambiguous that the solo continued.

Nothing you write into a score, no matter how obvious, will make you look a fool. Players love to be reassured by the obvious.

What would be embarrassing would be if you missed out some instruction you thought obvious, but which turned out not to be.

Only mildly embarrassing, actually. It happens to arrangers all the time!

31 The word *fine* (pronounced 'fee-nay') is Italian for 'end'.
It's not necessary to put it in. I thought I'd show it to you in case you
wanted to be flash like me!

YES TODAY

D. Runswick

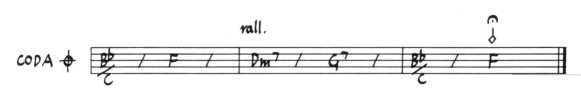

Appendix I: Time-saving Shortcuts for Writers

1 Repeat signs

If the music repeats itself, don't write it out twice!

Three   blind   mice,   See   how   they   run,

2 First- and second-time boxes

If the music repeats, but has a slightly different ending the second time, use first- and second-time boxes.

See   how   they   run,   run,   They   all   ran af - ter the

Second time through, the player jumps from the end of bar 3 (above) straight to the second-time box.

You can have first-, second- and third-time boxes if you need them. And fourth-, and so on – though it all gets rather hard to read; so not too many!

3 Different loudness on repeat

If you want the music soft the first time through and louder the second time, put both markings in order, separated by a comma.

mf, p

4 D𝄋 (dal 𝄋 or dal segno) al ⊕, DC (da capo) al ⊕

Use these signs to repeat a long section from an earlier part of the arrangement.

D𝄋 (often called 'the sign') instructs the player or singer to look back through the arrangement for the 𝄋 which you've planted:

– and to jump back to that point, playing or singing on until they reach the ⊕ sign.

They then jump *forward* to the coda (ending):

CODA ⊕

DC takes you back to the very beginning.

In this case you don't have to write anything at the place you want people to jump back to – they know it's the beginning!

You can have ordinary repeat signs within a section covered by a D𝄋 or DC.

If you don't want a repeat done when you're going through the passage after the D𝄋 or DC, write:

(or, *No repeat on DC*)

5 Adding or subtracting instruments on repeat, D𝄋 or DC.

Say you decide, before or after you've laid out the score or lead sheet, that you want an instrument to play *only on one of the times through*: mark as follows:

To make them play first time only:

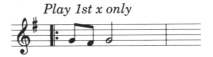

To make them play second time only:

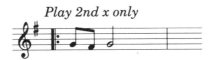

To make them play before the 𝄋 only:

To make them play after the sign only:

6 Single bar repeats, two bar repeats, etc.

The ⅞ sign means play or sing the last bar again. You can keep writing it for as long as you want the same bar repeated.

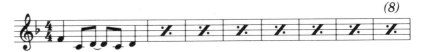

When there are a lot of these repeats, it helps the player if you mark the total number over the final bar (including the original, written-out bar).

This means play or sing the last *two* bars again.

This means play or sing the last *four* bars again.

This means repeat the last bar to make *eight times* in all. You can do it for any number of repeats, of course.

7 Simile (or sim. for short)
This means 'carry on in a similar way'.

You can use it, as above, on a drum part, putting slashes on every beat afterwards.

You can use it to avoid having to write out annoying things like staccato dots for several pages.

You can put it in a guitar or keyboard part to tell the player to continue a similar pattern through the chord changes.
    And in many other ways. It's a useful little word!

8 PLAY 8 BARS, PLAY 12 BARS, etc.

For drum and percussion parts when you just want them to carry on playing·

If you are using rehearsal letters (*) in your arrangement (*and you should*!), write in the number of bars until the next letter, mark the letter, and carry on.

This shortcut only works in parts, not in scores.

9 Chords col (see also Chapter 15, 27–28)

In a score, you can save copying out a chord sequence (*) several times with this method.

Write out the chords once (generally in the part with the stave highest in the score), then put 'chords col [that instrument]' and a wavy line along the other staves, for as long as the chords are the same.

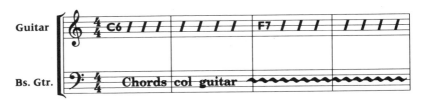

10 Reference bars (see also Chapter 15, 21–26)

For score-writing ONLY! Do not do this in parts!

To save score-writing time, you can indicate that a bar copied out earlier in any part is to be played again.

Find the earlier bar which is the same and write its rehearsal letter and bar-number inside a circle.

So the second bar of letter C is C2. (C2) is what you write in the new bar.

If more than one instrument is repeating an earlier bar, draw a wavy line down from the reference through all the instruments:

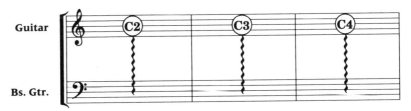

11 Multiple reference bars (see also Chapter 15, 25–26)

You can refer back to a whole section with just one reference bar.

This only works if the whole arrangement does a sixteen-bar repeat.

12 Repeated quavers or semiquavers on the same note

A slash through the stem of a minim or crotchet, or above (or below) a semibreve, tells the player to play quavers up to the value of that note.

Two slashes means semiquavers.

If there is a long series of these, it is usual to write out the first group.

13 A straight line to continue a given scale
This is mostly used for strings and harp.

You can write this for an upward or downward scale.

Write out the first octave of the scale in demi-semiquavers (so you've given the player all the notes), then draw a thick line up to the top note you want played.

The length of the last note plus the rests at the end of the bar show where the scale should finish.

If you want the scale to finish at the end of the bar, don't put any rests in.

The scale can of course last for more than one bar. Draw it graphically, the length you want it.

14 and tacet (for copying parts only)
(*Tacet*, pronounced 'tassit', means 'do not play'.)

You may find, when part-copying, that an instrument's music stops a long way before the end.

The rest of the part, fully copied out, would look something like this:

There's no need to copy this – the player doesn't need it, even for rehearsal. (The bandleader says, 'OK, from letter ⬚E⬚.' The player knows that she or he is not in that bit.)

Just put '*and tacet*' after the last bar in which the instrument does play.

Appendix 2: Chord Symbols

Chord symbols are easy enough to learn, but there are one or two tricky little rules which might catch you out.

True to the spirit of this book I'll give you the hard info first and deal with the theory of it all at the end of the chapter.

The chords

1 **Here are the most usual chords, in their simplest voicings, in four keys.**

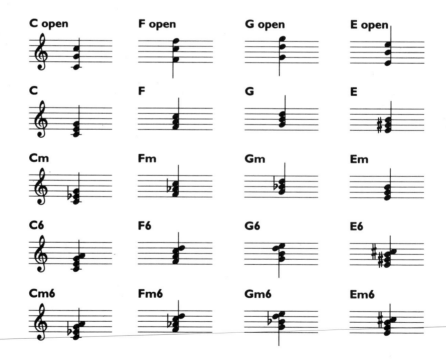

The chord sequence

First method: without melody

2 Write the chords within the stave.* Put the first chord at the beginning of the first bar and fill in the remaining beats of the bar with slashes. Write a bar-line.
Your first bar looks like this:

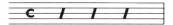

3 Add more bars in the same way. Put a slash for every beat where the chord *doesn't* change, and put a chord symbol wherever it *does*.

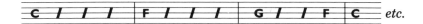

So every bar (in $\frac{4}{4}$) will have a total of four things in it, either chord symbols or slashes. (In $\frac{3}{4}$ there are a total of three things, in $\frac{5}{4}$ five, one for each beat of the bar.)

Some bars may have chord-changes on every beat, some bars may be full of slashes. **You don't have to repeat a chord at the beginning of the next bar if it doesn't change.**

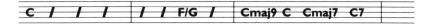

4 If a chord changes on a half-beat, draw the stems of two quavers, with the new chord under the second stem:

5 If you want the player to do a particular rhythm, mark it in stems above the stave.
(Use diamonds on the stems for notes longer than a crotchet.)

* Of course you can write a chord sequence on a piece of blank (non-music) paper if you wish. The example in **3** will then look like this:

6 If you want the player *not to play* at certain times, mark rests in the part exactly as in conventional notation.
You can of course start the part with rests if you wish.

etc.

7 If you want the same chord-change bar after bar, write the 'same again' sign in those bars.

is the same as

– and takes far less time to write!

If you're writing lots of bars the same again, number the last one for the benefit of the player.

8 You can write 'same again' over two bars.

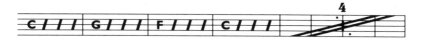

– or three or four bars:

9 Construct the part as you would any other, with rehearsal letters, repeat signs, dal segno, coda, cresc, dim, rall, etc., etc. See the example part at the start of Appendix 1.

Second method: with melody

10 You may wish to give the tune of your arrangement with the chords.
This is useful in

Lead sheets (*)

Head arrangements (*)

Keyboard or guitar parts

To do this simply write out the tune, then add a chord symbol above any note where the chord changes.

Do not write slashes. They're not needed.

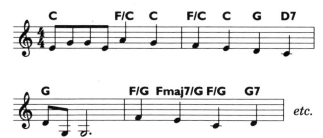

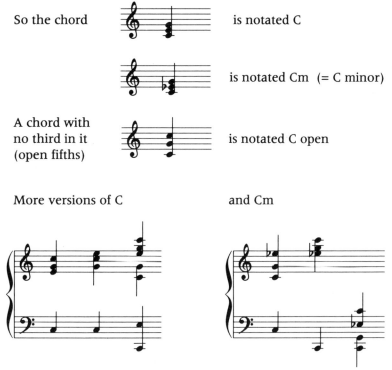

The theory

11 Chord symbols are based on (built up from) simple major and minor chords.

So the chord [music] is notated C

[music] is notated Cm (= C minor)

A chord with no third in it (open fifths) [music] is notated C open

More versions of C   and Cm

[music]

NB Some people notate C minor as C– (minor = minus). I advise against this because some other people notate C♭9 as C–9 (see 25 below). This stupid confusion has never been sorted out by the professionals, and players reading a part have to ask the

arranger which one she or he means! Since a good, unambiguous notation exists, I recommend you use it.

More complex chords are notated according to how they relate to the simple major and minor chords.

 is notated C⁶

12 The rule is, count up the scale from doh.

 therefore

is C⁶. A chord symbol always means '*doh, me and soh, plus* this number in the scale'.

So

More versions of C⁶

So as you see above, once you've got the notes in your chord (*doh, me and soh*, plus this number) you can spread them about how you like.

13 The chord's name-note (in this case C) must always be the bass-note.
For exceptions to this see **29** below.
   This rule is bent when guitar players play from chord symbols, because the guitar can't always manage the bass-note as well as the upper one. But it still applies in theory (the player *imagines* the bass-note and hopes the bass-player will supply it). So always write chords for the guitar *as if* they will play the bass-note.

14 The seventh is normally considered to be flat.

So C⁷ means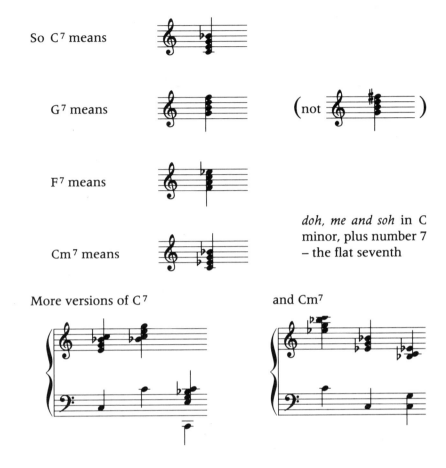

G⁷ means   (not   )

F⁷ means

Cm⁷ means

doh, me and soh in C minor, plus number 7 – the flat seventh

More versions of C⁷   and Cm⁷

15 The true seventh of the major scale (*te*) is called the major seventh.

So to show   as a chord symbol you write Cᵐᵃʲ⁷.

16 Note that the 'maj' is written *above and to the right*, as well as the 7.

Some versions of F ᵐᵃʲ⁷   and G ᵐᵃʲ⁷

7 In minor keys the seventh of the *major* scale is also called the major seventh and notated.

(In other words, the same rule as for major chords.)

   is Cm maj7 (C minor, major seventh)

Now you see the importance of putting the 'maj' above and to the right! Cmmaj7 would just be confusing – which bit of the chord is minor, which major? These symbols have to be read quickly and accurately by the players.

Some versions of Fm maj7   and Gm maj7

18 With both C⁶ and Cm⁶ the sixth is the major scale one.

The minor scale sixth is notated C♭6 and Cm♭6. (NB don't confuse this chord with the augmented one, see next paragraph.)

19 The following chord is called 'augmented'. Notate C+ or C aug.

The word 'augmented' refers to the fact that the fifth of the chord (G) is sharpened (augmented) to G♯.

The difference between C♭6 and C+ is that C♭6 has *both* the true fifth and the flat sixth in it. C+ has no true fifth.

Of the two chords, C+ is by far the more common.

20 The following chord is called 'diminished'. Notate Cdim.

It is called 'diminished' on the same principle as 'augmented': the fifth of the chord (G) is flattened (diminished) to F♯.

Diminished chords are sometimes notated C°. I personally don't like this notation. It's not very common.

Diminished chords are always endless strings of minor thirds, starting on any note.

Some versions of Fdim   and Gdim

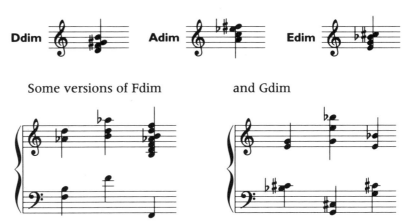

21 The following chord is called 'minor 7, flat five'. Notate Cm$^{7♭5}$.

It's quite logical: C minor + the seventh + the flattened fifth.

This chord is sometimes called 'C half-diminished' (it has only one note different from a diminished chord).

Some versions of Fm$^{7♭5}$ and Gm$^{7♭5}$

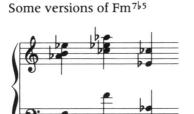

22 Going outside the octave, you can add a ninth to your chord.

23 C⁹ is a C⁷ with an added ninth.
In other words, the seventh is always flat.

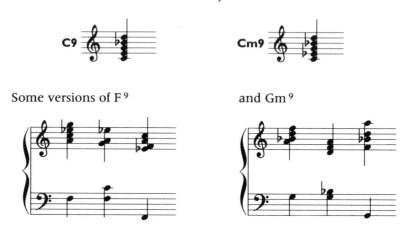

24 C^maj9 is a C^maj7 with an added ninth.
In other words it is the *seventh* which is major.

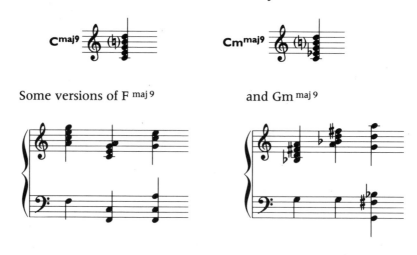

25 C⁷♭⁹ is a C⁷ with a flat ninth.

You can also notate these chords C♭9 and Cm♭9. I prefer the more complete version.

NB Some people notate C♭9 as C−9. I advise against this because some other people notate Cm as C− (see 11 above). This stupid confusion has never been sorted out by the professionals, and players reading a part have to ask the arranger which one she or he means! Since a good, unambiguous notation exists, I recommend you use it.

Some versions of F$^{7♭9}$ and Gm$^{7♭9}$

26 **The following chord is called C seven, sharp nine, *or* C seven, flat ten. Notate C$^{7♯9}$ or C$^{7♭10}$.**

Some versions of F$^{7♯9}$ and G$^{7♭10}$

27 **The following chord is called a 'suspended fourth'. Notate C^{sus4}.** This chord has no third in it.

The reason it's called a suspended fourth is (or *ought to be*) lost in the ancient history of classical music. It just means there's a fourth instead of a third in the chord.

Some versions of F ^{sus 4}   and G ^{sus 4}

28 Combination chords. Use any combination of symbols to describe the complex chord you've dreamed up.

We've already done this above with Cm $^{7\flat5}$, C $^{7\flat5}$ and C $^{7\sharp9}$.

The rule for the order of the symbols is

Key-note	e.g. C
Minor if it applies	e.g. Cm
Dim or aug if it applies	e.g. C $^+$
Sixth if it applies	e.g. Cm ^{6}
Which seventh it is	e.g. C $^{+\,maj\,7}$
Sus four or flat five if it applies	e.g. C ^{7sus4}, Cm $^{7\flat5}$
Numbers outside the octave	e.g. C $^{+\,maj\,7\,9}$

C $^{+\,maj\,7\,9}$ would work out as

Some complex chords in F   and Gm

29 'Pedals'

Sometimes a chord gets so complex that it's easier to describe it in terms of a simpler chord *over* a bass-note (pedal-note).

The following chord is B♭/C (say 'B♭ over C')

Using the ordinary notation this would have to be something like C ^no 3rd no 5th 9 11^. The 'pedal' notation helps by simplifying into two easily understood elements. It additionally helps keyboard players, who can do the chord-shape with their right hand and the bass-note with their left.

Some versions of chords over F   and over G

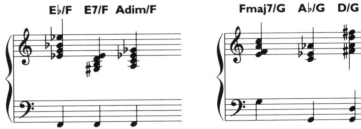

30 More complex chords can often be described in more than one valid way.

for instance 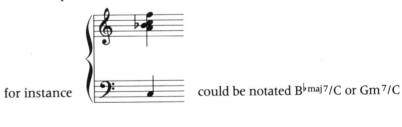 could be notated B♭maj7/C or Gm7/C

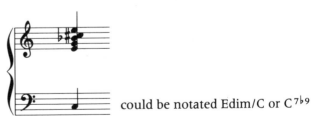 could be notated Edim/C or C7♭9

In such cases you can choose which notation to use.

Glossary

If the definition given here is not full enough, or if the word you want is not listed, try the index.

Percussion instruments are not given here. They are listed alphabetically in Chapter 8.

a capella	Without rhythm section (the original Italian means 'like in church').
acoustic	Describes any unamplified sound.
arco	(Of stringed instruments) played with the bow.
arpeg.	Play arpeggios.
arpeggiated	Made up of arpeggios.
arpeggio	Broken chord – the notes of a chord played one at a time, upwards or downwards. (Pronounced 'arpejyo'.)
articulation	The distinctive way in which an instrument moves from one note to the next.
attack	The way a note starts (hard attack/soft attack, etc.).
amp	Amplifier.
axe	Musicians' general term for their instrument.
backing	Accompaniment.
backing group	The group that accompanies a soloist.
backing track	A pre-recorded accompaniment.
backing vocals	Voices accompanying a soloist.
balalaika	A guitar-like instrument from Russia.
ballad	A slow song.
banjolele	A cross between a ukelele and a banjo.
bassline	The notes played by the bass instrument in a rhythm section; or by the bass instrument in an a capella group; or by the left hand of a keyboard.
b.d. or BD	Bass drum.
beaters	Percussionists' sticks of various shapes and sizes.
bebop	A style of jazz current in the 1940s and '50s, still used by some players today.
blue-grass	A style of American folk music.
blues	1) A style of playing. 2) A feeling of sadness. 3) A musical form of twelve bars.
bottleneck	A metal tube used by guitarists for a sliding sound.

bouzouki	A guitar-like instrument from Greece.
brass	All the instruments in the trumpet family.
break	1) Solo.
	2) The middle 'b' section of an 'aaba' form.
	3) The part of a voice-range where the change comes from chest to head voice.
	4) The part of a clarinet's range where the change comes between lower and upper registers.
bright/brite	1) Of tempo: fast.
	2) Of sound: piercing, toppy.
bucket mute	A brass mute.
bvox	Backing vocals (pronounced 'beevox').
chest voice	The powerful lower range of the human voice.
choral	For a choir.
chordal	Using chords.
chord symbols	A way of notating harmonies. See Appendix 2.
chorus	1) To chorus: make the sound appear twice as thick, as if played by two instruments in unison.
	2) A chorus: once through the tune or chord sequence.
	3) A choir.
chorusing	The effect of making the sound thicker.
chromatic	Using all the twelve notes of the octave.
clavinet	A brash, twangy sound made by some synths.
coda	Ending.
col	Italian for 'with'.
combo	Short for combination; a group or band.
comp	Short for 'accompany'.
concert pitch	The pitch to which synths and pianos are pre-tuned. Technically, middle C is tuned to 256 Hz.
con sord	With mute.
contact mic	A microphone which picks up sound from an instrument it is touching.
counter-melody	A secondary tune which is played behind the main one.
cover version	An arrangement or performance which is a straight copy of a well-known version of the same song.
cue	A sign given by the bandleader.
dal 𝄋	(Dal segno) go from the sign.
damp	Stop an instrument (esp. percussion) ringing.
DC	(Da capo) go from the beginning.
delay	The electronic repeating of a note one or more times. Not to be confused with reverb.
diatonic	Using only the notes of the major or minor scale.
distort	The deliberate or accidental overloading of an amplified sound.
dotted feel	The beat divided into triplets.
double	Play two or more instruments (not all at once!).
double feel	Style of playing which makes the music feel twice as fast.
double-reed	The family of instruments containing the oboe, cor anglais and bassoon.
double stave	Two staves joined by a 'bow' bracket, as in piano music.
double-stopping	Playing two or more notes at once on an instrument of the violin family.

drum machine	An electronic box for playing synthesized drum patterns.
drum pattern	The basic thing the drummer chooses to play throughout any piece.
dynamics	The loudness or softness of the music (a low dynamic would be *piano*, a high dynamic would be *forte*).
echo	A woolly word it would be better for you not to use. It is imprecisely applied to both reverb and delay; and it's better to use one of these proper words, which are unambiguous.
electric piano	An electric keyboard with all the features (touch, sustain, etc.) of a piano. It doesn't sound much like a piano. When the same sound is made by a synth it's called a digital electric piano.
electronic	Using electricity to produce or alter the actual notes of an instrument.
electronics	The theory and art of electronic instruments.
ensemble	1) A group. 2) Part of an arrangement featuring the whole group.
envelope	1) The rise and fall of any aspect of a sound, shown as a graph. 2) A guitar or synth effect.
falsetto	The high, piping part of a man's voice.
feedback	A whistling sound made if you turn an amp up too far. Usually produced accidentally and got rid of as quickly as possible, it is also used deliberately by guitarists as an effect.
feel	The style in which the music is played; therefore the way it 'feels'.
f-holes	The f-shaped holes in the belly of some stringed instruments.
fills	Melodic and/or rhythmic patterns used to fill a gap in the music.
filter-sweep	An effect which changes a sound as it is played, 'sweeping' up and down from dull to bright.
fine	Italian for 'end' (pronounced 'fee-nāy').
fingerboard	The part of a stringed instrument which the player fingers with the left hand.
first-time box	A way of manipulating repeat signs. See Appendix 1.
flange	A guitar or synth effect, giving a rippling sweep different from phasing or vibrato.
fluttertongue	On brass and reeds, a way of getting a tremolando effect.
form	The shape of a tune or piece.
fretboard	The fingerboard of a fretted instrument.
fretless	Without frets. This applies to some bass guitars.
frets	Metal strips across the fingerboards of guitars and similar instruments, which are used for pitching notes.
fretted	With frets.
full score	A longer name for a score.
function	This means quite simply, something that an instrument does: for instance, the loop (repeat) function on a drum machine makes the drum pattern repeat; the load function on a synth makes the sounds load into the memory, etc.
fx	Abbreviation of 'effects'.

gated reverb	An fx where reverb is added to a sound but cut off short.
gig	A concert or club appearance by a person or band.
glissando, gliss	A slide from one note to another; in keyboard or harp music, a fast run up or down.
gospel	Black American church music; very rhythmic.
graphic	Using picture-like notation.
hammering-down	A guitarist's technique. After playing one note you finger the next very hard (hammer-down) without picking it with your other hand.
harmon	A brass mute.
harmonics	Pure-toned high notes available on most acoustic instruments.
harmonies	Chords.
harmonizing	Electronically adding a second note at a predetermined interval.
head	The opening tune.
head arrangement	In jazz, an arrangement based on the opening tune and the chord sequence.
head voice	The lighter upper range of the human voice.
hillbilly	A style of American folk music.
hip-hop	A style of pop music.
horn	(Apart from instruments with this name) a nickname for any blowing instrument; occasionally, any instrument.
improvise	1) Make it up as you go along. 2) Solo over a chord sequence (*).
interval	The distance between two notes: C up to D is a second, C up to G is a fifth (work it out); C to E is a major third, C to E♭ is a minor third, etc.
intro	Introduction.
kit	All the instruments played by the drummer, plus the sticks, the stool, etc.
LA	Usually Latin-American (not Los Angeles!)
Latin	South-American-style music or instruments.
lead guitar	The guitar which plays the melody and takes solos.
lead sheet	A written copy of an arrangement which gives the melody, words, chords and routine in a specially abbreviated form.
lead trumpet	1) The highest trumpet in the section. 2) A high-note specialist trumpeter.
lead vocal	The main voice in a song.
legato	Played smoothly. [Pronounced 'legā-to'. The Italian for liver, however, is pronounced 'fē-gato'.]
licks	Scraps of melody, rhythm or bassline habitually used by a particular player.
loop	A section of music repeated over and over in a sequencer. From the old analogue 'tape loop'.
LV	Let vibrate.
lyrics	The words of a song.
lyricist	The person who writes the words of a song.
mallets	Percussion beaters.
mech fade	(Mechanical fade) the fade-out at the end of many records.

metronome	A ticking machine to tell you the speed of the music in beats per minute.
MIDI	A way of connecting electronic instruments and computers so that they play one another.
mic	Microphone.
mod, mod-wheel	Modulation. The mod-wheel on a synth when turned generally produces wobble of some sort.
MOR	Middle-of-the-road; easy-listening music.
multitrack	To record on a machine with many tracks, allowing for overdubs afterward.
mute	An add-on device for making an acoustic instrument play softer. It also alters the instrument's tone.
notate	Write down as music.
notation	The way you write down music.
nylon-strung	With strings made of nylon.
offbeat	In a $\frac{4}{4}$ bar, beats 2 and 4.
open string	A string played at the pitch to which it is tuned (i.e., not fingered).
operetta	Light opera, moving towards the musical.
oud	Guitar-like Arab instrument.
overdub	Record a new part on to tape or disk without erasing what you've already recorded.
part	1) An instrument or voice's line within an arrangement. 2) An instrument or voice's written-out music.
passage-work	Repeated patterns.
pastiche	Music which deliberately copies or apes another style.
pattern	A unit of music, say four notes or four bars, which is repeated again and again.
(pedal notes) (pedal tones)	1) Low notes 2) A drone.
pedal steel	A kind of stand-mounted electric guitar used mostly in Hawiian and country music. The notes are changed using a combination of pedals and a bottleneck.
phase, phasing	A guitar or synth effect giving the notes a subtle wobble, different from vibrato or flanging.
phrase	As in speech, a group of notes which naturally form a unit.
phrase-marks	The lines (like slurs) in the music which tell the player or singer how to do the phrasing.
phrasing	The way a player puts the music into 'sentences and paragraphs'.
pick	1) Play single-note patterns on a guitar. 2) The pick is the implement with which the guitar is often plucked.
pickups	Electronic sensors on guitars, etc., which 'pick up' the sound and deliver it to an amplifier.

pitch	Note; notes.
pitch-bend	Sliding sharper or flatter on a note.
pizz	Pizzicato.
pizzicato	Plucked, not bowed (of stringed instruments).
plunger	A brass mute giving a wah-wah effect.
ponticello, sul ponticello	Bow a stringed instrument close to the bridge, giving a thin, glassy effect.
preset	A setting or sound in the memory of an electronic instrument, which can be called up at the touch of a button.
program	A set of instructions fed into a computer or synth.
range	The lowest and highest notes an instrument is able to play, or a voice to sing.
rap	Rhythmic talking over a beat.
reed	The part of a clarinet, sax, oboe, etc. which vibrates to produce the note (flutes don't have reeds, but they are still called 'reeds').
reeds	All the saxophone family, plus flutes and clarinets.
reference bars	A method of writing in the score to save time. See Appendix 1 or Chapter 15.
reggae	One style of Caribbean music.
register	One part of an instrument's range (high register, middle register, low register).
rehearsal letters	Letters of the alphabet written through a score or part so that at rehearsals players can agree where to go from.
reverb (Reverberation)	The electronic simulation of the sound music makes in a large room. It is confusing to call it 'echo', and wrong to call it 'delay'.
Rhodes	A name sometimes given to the electric piano, after the inventor of one widely used design.
rhythm guitar	The guitar which keeps the rhythm and chords going.
rhythm section	Guitar(s), keyboard(s), bass, drums and percussion.
rhythm track	The rhythm section parts of a tune, recorded.
riff	A repeated melodic fragment.
round and round	Keep repeating.
routine	A simple chart laying out the shape of an arrangement.
routining	Making a routine.
salsa	One style of South American music.
sampler	A synth which uses recorded sounds (samples) rather than synthesized ones.
,sampling	Recording sounds for use in a sampler.
scat	Nonsense words used by jazz singers.
score	1) A score is all the parts of an arrangement written down on the same page. 2) To score is to write down all the parts of your arrangement on the same page.
score-paper	Music paper with more than the usual number of staves, for writing out scores.
second-time box	A way of manipulating repeat signs. See Appendix 1.
section	A group of players of similar instruments (brass section, string section).

senza	Italian for 'without'.
sequence	A passage of music saved into a computer's or a synth's memory, which can be played back.
sequencer	A computerized device which creates and stores sequences.
shape	The way the notes in a chord are laid out; voicing.
signal processing	Adding an electronic effect to a sound.
sim	Short for simile.
simile	(Italian, pronounced 'similay') carry on in the same way.
sitar	An Indian and Pakistani instrument distantly related to the guitar.
slap bass	A highly percussive way of playing the bass guitar.
slap echo	A very fast single delay.
slur	1) Join two or more notes together smoothly. 2) The curved line in music which joins notes to be played in this way.
smear	On saxes, sliding between two notes.
solid-body	An electric guitar or bass which cannot be heard acoustically.
solo	1) The lead part. 2) An improvised passage
sord.	The mute (Italian: *sordino*)
stab	A hard, short sound.
standard	Any well-known song.
stave	The five lines of music writing.
steel-strung	With strings made of metal.
stop	1) Any sound on an electric organ. 2) Do any kind of stopping (see below).
stopping	1) Fingering a stringed instrument. 2) Inserting a hand into the bell of a french horn. 3) Muffling the sound of a guitar with the right hand.
straight mute	A brass mute.
strings	All the instruments of the violin family: violin, viola, cello, double bass.
strum	Specially on guitar: play a chord with one stroke of the fingers or pick.
sustain	1) The length of time a note lasts if you let it ring. 2) To sustain a note is to keep it sounding.
sustain pedal	A pedal used on keyboards to make the sound carry on after you take your hands away. The 'loud pedal' on a piano.
swing	Jazz style, dotted feel.
synth	Short for synthesizer. I use the word to mean any keyboard or other instrument which plays electronically produced sounds: including samplers, drum machines, MIDI guitar and wind controllers, rack-mounted signal generators, etc.
synthesis	The making of new sounds on a synth.
tabulature	Various systems of notation for guitars and similar instruments.
tacet	(Pronounced 'tassit') do not play.

take	An attempt at recording something. The first attempt is called take 1, the second take 2, etc. The take you finally use is called the master (a rather sexist way of talking, perhaps!)
tempo	The speed of the music, as given when you count it in ('A-one, two, one two three four').
texture	How you arrange the instruments or voices together (thin texture, thick texture, etc.).
theme	Tune.
tight	1) Well-disciplined 2) Precisely rhythmic.
timbre	Sound; tone quality.
tin mute	A brass mute.
touch	The strength with which a keyboard player hits the notes (hard touch, soft touch, etc.).
transpose	Put a note, melody or piece of music into a different key.
transposing instrument	An instrument whose written music has to be transposed. See Chapter 10.
trem	Tremolando.
tremolando	Trembling, shimmering.
tremolo	1) A wobble/pitch-bend device on some guitars. 2) The word is also sometimes used (incorrectly, but everybody does it) for tremolando.
trill	1) The fast alternation of two adjacent notes. 2) In percussion, a drum (or cymbal, tam-tam, etc.) roll.
tuned	Of percussion: playing pitched notes.
ukelele	A tiny Hawaiian four-stringed guitar.
unaccompanied	Played or sung completely on its own.
unison	Played or sung together at the same pitch.
untuned	Percussion instrument which doesn't play a pitched note.
vibrato	Fast wobble.
virtuoso	1) Brilliant (of playing or singing). 2) A brilliant player or singer.
voicing	1) The way a chord is laid out – its exact pitches. 2) Which instruments shall play each note of a chord.
wah-wah	An effect produced on brass instruments by using a plunger mute; similar effects can be achieved on guitars (with an fx box), on synths and by the voice.
walking	A style of bassline much used in jazz: one note on every beat.
wind controller	A dummy (noiseless) wind instrument that you can use to play a synth if you don't have keyboard skills.
x	Time, or times.

Index

Figures in italics refer to music illustrations.